FOODI MULTI-COOKER COOKBOOK

For Complete Beginners

THE PRESSURE COOKER THAT CRISPS.

Amazingly Easy & Delicious Foodi Multi-Cooker Recipes to Pressure Cook, Air Fry, Dehydrate and Many More.

By

Francis Michael

ISBN: 978-1-952504-30-3

DISCLAIMER

The information contained in this book is geared for educational and entertainment purposes only. Strenuous efforts have been made towards providing accurate, up to date and reliable complete information. The information in this book is true and complete to the best of our knowledge. Neither the publisher nor the author takes any responsibility for any possible consequences of reading or enjoying the recipes in this book. The author and publisher disclaim any liability in connection with the use of information contained in this book. Under no circumstance will any legal responsibility or blame be apportioned against the author or publisher for any reparation, damages, or monetary loss due to the information herein, either directly or indirectly.

Table of Contents

BEEF & PORK RECIPES

FISH & SEAFOODS

INTRODUCTION

In recent times, a new kitchen appliance emerged and is gaining more popularity and patronage. The name of the new appliance is called Ninja Foodi. This unit is a combination of both pressure cooker and air fryer. It combines the speed of a pressure cooker with that of crisping action of an air fryer to give your food a nice and Tender-Crisp Technology.

The Ninja Foodi can cook quick meals with a nice texture and your food could be on your table in no distant time. This means Ninja Foodi has the capacity to cook food faster. It makes a healthier cooking by combining whole ingredients together to make sumptuous meal. Ninja Foodi has a kind of innovation which makes it different from other cooking appliances. It gives you a Tender-Crisp food from one unit. Another unique feature of the Ninja Foodi is that it can be used as a steamer, slow cooker, oven and roaster etc.

Ninja Foodi is a nice all-in-one product which is so unique and excellent. It performs an excellent task of pressure cooking and air frying. However, it also performs a similar function unlike the Instant Pot and other electric pressure cookers. In terms of the physical outlook, the Ninja has a beautiful display window which shows you what is happening in the pot. It also shows hint to lock the lid and the remaining cooking time. There is a blue light on the display window which rotates when Ninja is still on pressure but stops rotating when Ninja's pressure is reached.

Meaning of Ninja Foodi

This is a new trending kitchen appliance. It is a pressure cooker that crisps. Ninja has a 6.5qt pressure cooker along with a 4qt Cook & crisp basket for the Tender Crisp (this is an Air Fryer function). It is correct to say that the Ninja Foodi is an Air Fryer, a pressure cooker and a dehydrator. The appliance allows you to turn ingredients that are tough to become tender, juicy and full of flavor.

It cooks food as faster as you could expect. The Ninja Foodi is usually called and ultimate Air Fryer due to its crisping lid that is powerful. Ninja Foodi is a unit that uses super-heated steam to put moisture and flavor into your foods. The crisping lid releases hot air all around your food for a crispy result. The Ninja Foodi is a combination of 4 in 1 appliance which includes: A pressure cooker, dehydrator, slow cooker and air fryer.

Benefits of Using the Ninja Foodi

There are lots of benefits you can get from using this appliance. The benefit that outweighs other appliances is that it does not require you to flip the fries over to the other side many times compared to other pressure cookers. You may only shake the fries on halfway to cooking time for a proper cooking. The benefits are shown below:

1. **Crispy Wings**

Start cooking your chicken or turkey wings even in haste with the pressure cooker mode. When the normal cooking is done, switch to the air fryer to get that hot air circulating all around the wings and gives you a crispy result. You can combine with any sauce of your choice for your dinner or as an appetizer.

2. **Baked Macaroni and Cheese**

This unit allows you to cook macaroni and cheese and gives you a crispy result. When you are done with the normal cooking, you can swap to the Air Fryer mode for that crispy golden brown topping that you would get when baked.

3. **Scalloped Potatoes**

Everybody loves a eating creamy scalloped potatoes. The unit tenders your potatoes and then with the air fryer for a crispy result. Ninja Foodi allows you to cook all kinds of food unlike other units like air fryer or pressure cooker.

4. **Pressure cook and crisp**

Ninja Foodi enables you to pressure cook something and then make it crispy. This crispiness makes the chicken you cook not to require that you bring the chicken to the broiler. Everything can stay neat and nice.

Cooking things at once is very beneficial and helpful to Ninja Foodi users because it is not time consuming cooking a healthy food with the unit. The parts are easy to clean and it has a large cooking capacity.

Function Keys of Your Ninja Foodi

Ninja Foodi comes with many buttons for optimum operation of the unit which includes steam, slow cook, pressure cook, sear/sauté button, air crisp, broil, bake /roast and keep warm, buttons respectively. It also has buttons for temperature and time controls, start/stop button. The buttons and their functions are shown below:

1. **Pressure cook:**

This button helps you to cook your meal up to 4 hours using high or low pressure. As earlier said, it is possible to adjust the cooking time to 1 minute increment for 1 hour. When the time is up, you may increase the time to 5 minutes and begin to cook up to 4 hours. Hence you can make a whole lot of meals.

2. **Air Crisp:**

This function gives you an opportunity to adjust the temperature to either 300°F or 400°F and also adjust to increase the cooking time to 2 minutes for the highest cooking time of 1 hour. The air crisp button is used in cooking many dishes like chicken tenders, French fries etc. Pressure cooked food can be crisp using this button.

3. **Bake/Roast:**

This setting in the Ninja is good for making roasted meats and baked foods. For this function, the Ninja Foodi uses the air-frying lid. There is no problem if you set the cooking time to 1 minute increment for 1 hour. When the time is up, you may increase the time to 5 minutes and begin to cook up to 4 hours. After the hour mark, you can increase the time in five-minute increments and cook for up to four hours.

4. **Steam:**

It is possible to steam your veggies and other meals by putting the pressure lid on the Ninja Foodi with the sealing valve in the vent position.

5. **Slow cook:**

This button also makes use of the pressure lid with the sealing valve in the vent position. It is possible for you to slow cook low or slow cook high. The cooking time can also be adjusted to 15 minutes increment for up to 12 hours. It is advisable to use the slow cook mode when cooking meals like stews, soup or pot roasts.

6. **Sear/Sauté:**

This button on the Ninja Foodi does not make use of the lid. It only has a temperature setting of 5 different modes respectively. These includes: medium, medium-high, high, low or medium-low, setting. Foods can be browned after cooking or before cooking. The button can also be used to make different kinds of sauces, gravies. This button functions the same as you would sear or sauté using your stovetop.

Ninja Foodi Pressure Releasing Methods

This process is ideal for stopping all cooking process in order to avoid the food getting burnt. Foods like corn or broccoli etc. are ideal for this pressure releasing. There are two types of pressure release namely: Quick and natural pressure release.

1. **How to do a Ninja Foodi Quick Release**

Immediately the cooking time is up, keep the venting knob on Venting Position to enable Ninja Foodi quickly release the pressure inside the pressure cooker. To release all the pressure, it normally takes some few minutes. Before you open the lid, wait until the valve drops.

2. **How to do a Ninja Foodi Natural Release**

Immediately the cooking time is up, you have to wait until the valve drops and the lid is opened. In order to make sure all the pressure is released before opening the lid, keep the venting knob on Venting Position. This particular pressure release technique normally takes about 10 – 25 minutes but it depends on the amount of food in your cooker. To do the 10 – 15 minutes pressure release, when the cooking time is up, wait 10 – 15 minutes before moving the Venting Knob from Sealing Position to Venting Position so as to enable the remaining pressure to be released. Do not fail to wait for the floating valve to drop before you open the lid.

Steps on How to Use Your Ninja Foodi

This appliance is a very friendly and easy-to-use kitchen unit.

For Ninja Foodi pressure cooker:

1. Always put your foods in the inner pot of the Ninja Foodi or you put your food in the Air Fryer basket. This is basically good for meats.

2. Press the power on function.

3. Close lid in place. Do not put the one that is attached.

4. Set the top steam valve to seal position and press the pressure function.

5. Adjust the temperature to either high or low using the + or − buttons respectively.

6. Set the cooking time using the + or − buttons.

7. Press Start button.

8. The Ninja Foodi will take a little time to reach pressure and then will count the number of minutes until it reaches zero minute.

For Ninja Foodi Air Fryer:

1. Make use of the lid that is attached.

2. Place the Air Fryer cooking basket inside the Ninja Foodi inner pot.

3. Place your food inside the cooking basket.

4. Lock the attached lid and switch on the Ninja Foodi by pressing the button at the bottom.

5. Push the air crisp button.

6. Select the temperature you want to use by pressing the + and − buttons.

7. Set the cooking time by pressing the + and − buttons.

8. Select start button.

Useful Tips & Tricks for Using Your Ninja Foodi

It is pertinent to inquire to know how to properly use a new appliance you bought. Ninja Foodi come with 2 distinct lids. One is for the electric pressure cooker while the other one is for the Air Fryer lid. It is possible to use both lids in on food. Immediately the pressure cooker is done, remove the pressure cooker lid and put the Air Fryer lid. This helps to crisp your food. Every new kitchen appliance you get comes with an operational manual to guide you on the proper usage of the unit. Below are some few tips for the proper usage of your Ninja Foodi:

1. Whenever you want to spray cooking spray on the inner pot of your Ninja Foodi, do not use aerosol cooking spray.
2. Try to use the recommended amount of water or broth if you are using the pressure cooking button. Wrong usage of water may not give you the desired result.
3. When you are not using your Ninja Foodi, unplug from any power source so as to avoid the appliance switch on by itself even when you did not press the power on button.
4. It is not advisable to use your Ninja Foodi on your stove top. This can easily damage the unit.

Ninja Foodi Troubleshooting Tips

Every electronic appliance sometimes has trouble shooting or shows a faulty message on the display. Below are some of the major trouble shooting or problems you could find on your Ninja Foodi.

1. My appliance is taking a long time to come to pressure. Why?

It is important to know how long it takes your Ninja Foodi to come to pressure. Base on a particular temperature you choose, cooking time may vary. Temperature of the cooking pot at the moment of cooking including the amount of ingredients also makes cooking time to vary. If the cooking time is taking a longer time than necessary, make sure your silicone ring is fully seated and flush against the lid, make sure the pressure lid is fully closed and set the pressure release valve to seal position.

2. Why is the cooking time counting slowly?

You have to make sure you set the time correctly. Check if you did not use hours instead of minutes. Note that the HH stands for hours while the MM stands for minutes on the display window respectively. You can increase or decrease the cooking time.

3. How do I know when the appliance is pressurizing?

When the appliance is building pressure, the rotating lights will display on the display window. When you are using steam or pressure mode, light will rotate on the display screen. It means the appliance is preheating. Immediately the preheating process finishes, the normal cooking time starts counting.

4. When I'm using the steam mode, my unit is bringing out a lot of steam.

During cooking, steam releasing on the pressure release valve is normal. It is advisable to allow the pressure release valve in the vent position for Steam, Slow Cook, and Sear or Sauté mode.

5. Why can't I take off the pressure lid?

The Ninja Foodi has to be depressurized before the pressure lid can be opened. This is one of the safety measures put by the manufacturer. In order to do a quick pressure release, set the pressure release valve to the vent position. Immediately the pressure is released completely, the lid will be ready to open.

6. Do I need to lose the pressure release valve?

The answer is yes. You have to loosen the pressure release valve. It helps to circulate pressure through some release of small amount of steam while cooking is done for the result to be excellent.

Ninja Foodi Frequently Asked Questions and Answers

Question 1: Can I deep fry chicken with this appliance?

Answer: Yes it is possible. You can cook a chicken in your Ninja Foodi. This is a new modern way of cooking that can tender your food and progress to crisping the food using hot air and give you a crispy result.

Question 2: Can I Take My Ninja Pot from the Refrigerator and Put directly in the appliance?

Answer: Yes, you can do it if your pot was in the refrigerator.

Question 3: Can the Pot enter under the Broiler or the Oven?

Answer: Yes. It is possible but you have to be extra careful while putting or taking the pot out from the Ninja Foodi. It is only the lid that you do not need to put under the oven or the broiler.

Question 4: Can the Baking or cooking pan enter under the oven?

Answer: Yes. It is very possible and good to put the cooking pan under the oven. You just need to be careful while inserting the pan.

Question 5: Can I use the buffet settings to cook?

Answer: NO. It is not advisable to do that because the buffet function is just to keep temperature that is above 140°F when the food has been cooked to 165°F.

Question 6: What is the meaning of One-pot Meal Cooking?

Answer: These are important family meal that could be ready within 30 minutes time. The one pot helps in a quick clean up.

Question 7: What differentiate model op301 from model op305?

Answer: Model OP305 has the Dehydrate button while model OP301 has no dehydrate button. That's the major difference.

Question 8: Can you can food with Ninja Foodi?

Answer: No you will not be able to can food with this appliance. You can only do it if you have a pressure canner can.

Question 9: Why is the time beeper not beeping?

Answer: You can check the volume level.

Question 10: Can I put frozen pork loin in my Ninja Foodi?

Answer: Yes. It is possible to do that. Frozen foods can be cooked with this appliance.

Question 11: If the Ninja foodi displays watr, what is the meaning?

Answer: It means that you need to put more water into the Ninja Foodi. If at a point of putting more water and the error still show up, contact the customer care on 877-581-7375.

Question 12: Can meat and cheese vegetables be cooked with this appliance?

Answer: No. Ninja Foodi was not meant for canning of foods. So it will not work for you.

BREAKFAST RECIPES

Hash Brown Casserole

Preparation Time: 5 minutes

Cook Time: 30 minutes

Total Time: 35 minutes

Serve: 12

Ingredients:

- 6 Eggs

- 48 Oz. bag frozen hash browns

- ¼ Cup milk

- 1 Large onion

- 3 Tbsp. olive oil

- 1 Lbs. Ham

- ½ Cup cheddar cheese

Cooking Instructions:

1. Keep your Ninja Foodi on sauté mode. Put olive oil and chopped onion. Sauté for about 2 minutes.
2. Add the frozen hash browns and cook for 15 minutes at 350°F turning over to the other side while cooking time is halfway.
3. Whisk eggs and milk together, pour it on the hash browns and put meat.
4. Put the mixture into your Ninja Foodi and cook at 350°F for 10 minutes. Top with Cheddar cheese.
5. Serve and enjoy!!!

French Toast Casserole

Preparation Time: 5 minutes

Cook Time: 20 minutes

Total Time: 25 minutes

Serve: 6

Ingredients:

- 2 Tbsp. milk

- 1 Tbsp. cinnamon

- 2 Packs Grand's cinnamon rolls

- 4 Eggs

- 1 Tbsp. vanilla

Cooking Instructions:

1. Mix together eggs, milk and vanilla in a small mixing bowl.
2. Open the grand's cinnamon rolls and cut each of the dough into 4 places. Keep aside.
3. Put Cooking spray into your Ninja Foodi, put the dough in the cooking pan on top of the egg mixture.
4. Bake for about 20 minutes. Top with Syrup.
5. Serve and enjoy!!!

Starbucks Egg Bites

Preparation Time: 1 minute

Cook Time: 1 hour 30 minutes

Total Time: 1 hour 31 minutes

Serve: 1

Ingredients:

- 6 Eggs

- ¼ Cup Monterey jack cheese

- 6 4 Oz. mason jars

- ¼ Cup of milk or cream

- 3 Strips of bacon cooked

- ¼ Cup of Gruyere cheese

Cooking Instructions:

1. Preheat your oven to 350ºF degrees. Mix together eggs and milk.
2. Spray your Ninja Foodi cooking pan with nonstick cooking spray.
3. Put meat, gruyere cheese, egg mixture into each pan and top with Monterey jack cheese.
4. Cover the pans with lids, put them in the Ninja Foodi and cook for about 1 hour 30 minutes.
5. Serve and enjoy!!!

Red Velvet Waffles

Preparation Time: 5 minutes

Cook Time: 2 minutes

Total Time: 7 minutes

Serve: 3

Ingredients:

- ½ Cup of shortening

- 1 ½ Cups white sugar

- 4 Tbsp. red food coloring

- 1 Tsp. salt

- 1 Tsp. vanilla extract

- 1 Cup of buttermilk

- 2 ½ Cups of sifted all-purpose flour

- 1 ½ Tsp. baking soda

- 1 Tbsp. distilled white vinegar

- 2 Eggs

- 2 Tbsp. cocoa

Cooking Instructions:

1. In a small mixing bowl, beat eggs, shortening and 1 ½ cups of sugar. Mix thoroughly.
2. Prepare a red food coloring and a paste of cocoa. Pour into egg mixture, put 1 Tsp. vanilla, salt, buttermilk and mix thoroughly.
3. Put the flour and give it a good stir. Combine vinegar and soda. Fold into cake batter.
4. Put half cup of the mixture in the Ninja Foodi and cook for about 2 minutes. Repeat this until your cook everything.
5. Serve and enjoy!!!

Cracker Barrel Hash Brown Casserole

Preparation Time: 5 minutes

Cook Time: 2 minutes

Total Time: 7 minutes

Serve: 3

Ingredients:

- 1 30 Oz. bag of shredded hash browns

- 1 Cup of Colby cheese

- 1 Cup of cheddar cheese

- 1 Can of cream of chicken soup

- 1/2 Onion chopped

- salt

- 1 Can of cheddar cheese soup

- 1 Cup of sour cream

- pepper

Cooking Instructions:

1. Preheat your oven to 350ºF.
2. In a large mixing bowl, mix together all ingredients.
3. Pour into a baking pan and bake for 1 hour.
4. Serve and enjoy!!!

Cracked Out Tater Tot Breakfast Casserole

Preparation Time: 15 minutes

Cook Time: 50 minutes

Total Time: 1 hour 5 minutes

Serve: 8

Ingredients:

- 8 Eggs

- 2 Cups of milk

- 2 Lb. bacon

- 1 32 Oz. Bag frozen tater tots

- 1 (1 Oz.) Package Ranch dressing mixture

- 2 Cups of shredded cheddar cheese

Cooking Instructions:

1. Preheat oven to 350°F. Cook your bacon in a large skillet and then chop the bacon into small sizes after cooking.
2. Mix together chopped bacon, tater tots and cheeses in a small mixing bowl. Mix properly and pour into a greased baking pan.
3. Beat eggs and mix it together with Ranch mixture and milk. Mix properly and pour into bacon mixture.
4. Bake for 50 minutes.
5. Serve and enjoy!!!

Garlic Fries

Preparation Time: 10 minutes

Cook Time: 21 minutes

Total Time: 31 minutes

Serve: 4

Ingredients:

- 3 Tbsp. grated Parmesan Cheese

- ½ Cup of Water

- 2 Tbsp. Chopped Garlic

- 2 Tbsp. Fresh Parsley

- 4 Idaho Potatoes, sliced

- 4 Tbsp. Butter, melted

Cooking Instructions:

1. Put ½ cup of water into your Ninja Foodi. Put the potatoes; secure the lid keep pressure release valve to seal position.
2. Press Manual Low Pressure and set to cook for about 3 minutes. Mix together chopped garlic, parsley, melted butter and Parmesan.
3. When the pressure cooking time is up, open the lid and put garlic mixture on top of the fries. Lock the lid.
4. Cook at 400ºF for about 18 minutes. Flip them over while still cooking.
5. Serve and enjoy!!!

BBQ Ribs

Preparation Time: 2 minutes

Cook Time: 25 minutes

Total Time: 27 minutes

Serve: 8

Ingredients:

- 3 Cups of apple juice

- 1 Cup of BBQ Sauce

- 2 Racks of ribs

Cooking Instructions:

1. Set your Ninja Foodi to sauté and put juice. Put the ribs into the Ninja Foodi.
2. Lock the lid, select meat setting and set the Ninja Foodi to cook 25 minutes. When the cooking time is up, do a quick release.
3. Open the pressure lid. Close the crisping lid. Select air crisp and set the cooking temperature to 400°F for 15 minutes. Press Start/Stop button.
4. After 10 minutes of cooking time, open the crisping lid. Brush your BBQ sauce on the ribs. Lock the crisping lid and continue cooking for 5 minutes.
5. Serve and enjoy!!!

Lemon Custard Pie

Preparation Time: 20 minutes

Cook Time: 1 hour

Total Time: 1 hour 20 minutes

Serve: 6

Calories: 337 Kcal.

Ingredients:

- 1 Cup sugar

- 1 Cup of milk

- 2 Tsp. grated lemon peel

- 1 Unbaked pie pastry 9 inch

- 3 Tbsp. all-purpose flour

- 1/8 Tsp. salt

- ¼ Cup of lemon juice

- 1 Tbsp. butter softened

- 2 Eggs separated

Cooking Instructions:

1. Preheat oven to 325° F. Soften In a large bowl, beat the softened butter and sugar and blend properly.
2. Put one egg yolks at a time and blend properly. Put milk, flour and salt. Give it a good stir. Pour in the lemon juice and lemon peel.
3. Beat your egg whites in a large mixing bowl. Fold and put in your bowl of mixed ingredients. Pour the mixture into your pie shell.
4. Bake in your Ninja Foodi for about 1 hour.
5. Serve and enjoy!!!

Cherry Jam

Preparation Time: 10 minutes

Cook Time: 7 minutes

Total Time: 17 minutes

Serve: 20

Ingredients:

- Juice of ½ lemon

- 1 Package pectin

- ½ Cup of Honey

- 1 Lb. fresh cherries

Cooking Instructions:

1. Wash and chop your cherries. Put your honey and sauté for about 2 minutes.
2. When the honey is melted, put juice of half lemon, cherries and pectin powder. Give it a good stir.
3. Open the pressure lid. Close the crisping lid. Select air crisp and set the cooking temperature to 400°F for 5 minutes. Press Start/Stop button.
4. When the cooking time is up, do a natural pressure release for about 10 minutes.
5. Put the jam into jars and close it. You can put it in refrigerator if you so desire.
6. Serve and enjoy!!!

Breakfast Pockets

Preparation Time: 10 minutes

Cook Time: 10 minutes

Total Time: 20 minutes

Serve: 4

Ingredients:

- ½ Cup bacon, cooked

- ½ Cup cheddar cheese, shredded

- One box puff pastry sheets

- 5 Eggs

- ½ Cup sausage crumbles, cooked

Cooking Instructions:

1. Cook your eggs to look like scrambled eggs, if you so desire put meat to the egg mixture while you cook the mixture.
2. Lay puff pastry sheets on a cutting board and make a slice to have an equal rectangles using knife.
3. Scoop the egg mixture into half of the pastry rectangles. On top of the mixture, keep a pastry rectangle and seal with fork by pressing edges together.
4. Put breakfast pockets in Ninja Foodi and cook at 370°F for 10 minutes.
5. Serve and enjoy!!!

Oatmeal

Preparation Time: 5 minutes

Cook Time: 5 minutes

Total Time: 10 minutes

Serve: 4

Calories: 192kcal

Ingredients:

- 1 Cup of oats use steel oats

- 3 Tbsp. butter

- Pinch cinnamon

- 2 ½ Cup of water

- 1 Cup of apple skinned and diced

- 2 Tbsp. brown sugar

Cooking Instructions:

1. Put butter in your Ninja Foodi and melt it. Put oats, brown sugar, water, apples and cinnamon. Give it a good stir.
2. Open the pressure lid. Close the crisping lid. Select air crisp and set the cooking temperature to 400ºF for 5 minutes. Press Start/Stop button.
3. When the cooking time is up, do a quick pressure release.
4. Serve and enjoy!!!

Omelette in a Mug

Preparation Time: 5 minutes

Cook Time: 1 minute

Total Time: 6 minutes

Serve: 1

Calories: 281 kcal.

Ingredients:

- 1 Tbsp. bacon bits

- 2 Tbsp. cheese shredded

- 2 Eggs

- ½ Sausage link pre-cooked, diced

- 1 Mushroom sliced

Cooking Instructions:

1. Spray nonstick oil on a large mug. Beat the eggs into mug and mash with fork.
2. Put the remaining ingredients and give it a good stir.
3. Place in microwave for 1 minute if you are adding several ingredients.
4. Give it a good stir and spray cheese on the top.
5. Put in Microwave again for 20 seconds so that the cheese can melt.
6. Serve and enjoy!!!

Banana Bread

Preparation Time: 15 minutes

Cook Time: 45 minutes

Total Time: 1 hour

Serves: 24

Calories: 155 kcal

Ingredients:

- 3 Eggs

- ½ Cup of Mini chocolate chips

- 5 Bananas brown

- 1 Box cake mix

- ⅓ Coil

Cooking Instructions:

1. Crush bananas, put in all other ingredients except c chips and combine.
2. Wrap in chocolate chips. Put into Ninja Foodi for about 45 minutes.
3. Bake muffins for 18 min.
4. Serve and enjoy!!!

Breakfast Quinoa

Preparation Time: 5 minutes

Cook Time: 1 minute

Total Time: 6 minutes

Serves: 4

Calories: 310 kcal

Ingredients:

- 2 Tbsp. brown sugar

- 2 Tbsp. honey

- 1 ½ Cup of quinoa traditional white variety

- 2 ¼ Cup of water

- 1 Cup of blueberries

Cooking Instructions:

1. Put water and quinoa into your Ninja Foodi.
2. Close lid and set to sauté mode for 1 minute. Place into bowls.
3. Top with brown sugar, berries, and sprinkle with honey, put a bit of milk, half and half.
4. Serve and enjoy!!!

POULTRY RECIPES

Bacon

Preparation Time: 5 minutes

Cook Time: 8 minutes

Total Time: 13 minutes

Ingredient:

- Thick cut bacon

Cooking Instructions:

1. Fill the bottom of the Ninja Foodi ¼ of the way full with water.
2. Place a single layer of bacon in the Ninja Foodi. Set Ninja Foodi to sauté mode and cook for 8 minutes.
3. Monitor the bacon while cooking to achieve your desire.
4. Serve and enjoy!!!

Crispy Wings

Preparation Time: 5 minutes

Cook Time: 30 minutes

Total Time: 35 minutes

Serves: 4

Ingredient:

- 1 Stick Butter

- 2 ½ Lbs. Frozen Chicken Wings

- 1 Cup of water

- 1 Cup of Franks red hot sauce

Cooking Instructions:

1. Pour one cup of water into your Ninja Foodi and put wings in your fry basket.
2. Cook on high pressure for about 10 minutes and do a quick pressure release.
3. Open your pressure lid and use the air crisp lid and cook at 400°F for 20 minutes, flipping through while cooking.
4. Melt butter and combine together with hot sauce in a small mixing bowl. Coat the wings in the sauce.
5. Serve and enjoy!!!

Chicken Breast

Preparation Time: 5 minutes

Cook Time: 1 hour 30 minutes

Total Time: 1 hour 35 minutes

Serves: 4

Calories: 67 kcal

Ingredient:

- Seasoning of your choice

- Boneless Skinless Chicken

Cooking Instructions:

1. Preheat your Ninja Foodi. Spread your chicken and put them in a bag that can be sealed.
2. Put the chicken in your Ninja Foodi and cook for 1 hour 30 minutes.
3. Get the chicken out from the water bath and pat dry.
4. Put olive oil in a cast iron skillet and put the chicken breast. Cook for about 2 minutes on each side.
5. Serve and enjoy!!!

Buffalo and Ranch Wings

Preparation Time: 1 minute

Cook Time: 12 minutes

Total Time: 13 minutes

Serves: 4

Calories: 437 kcal

Ingredient:

- 3 Lbs. frozen chicken wings

- 1 Packet ranch seasoning

- 1 Cup of hot sauce

- ½ Cup of water

- 1 Stick butter melted

Cooking Instructions:

1. Put wings into your Ninja Foodi. Combine together ranch packet, butter, and hot sauce in a small mixing bowl.
2. Coat wings with the mixture and put ½ cup of water on the wings.
3. Cook on your Ninja Foodi on High pressure for about 12 minutes.
4. When the cooking time is up, do a quick release.
5. Remove wings and keep them on a baking sheet and then add broiler for about 2 minutes.
6. Serve and enjoy!!!

Root Beer Chicken Wings

Preparation Time: 5 minutes

Cook Time: 20 minutes

Total Time: 25 minutes

Serves: 1

Calories: 67 kcal

Ingredient:

- 2 Lbs. of chicken wings

- ¼ Cup of brown sugar

- ¼ Cup of root beer

- 1 Can of root beer

Cooking Instructions:

1. Put all your chicken wings into Ninja Foodi.
2. Put a can of root beer. Lock the lid and cook on high pressure for about 18 minutes.
3. When the cooking time is up, do a quick release and remove chicken wings.
4. In a small mixing bowl. Combine together ¼ cup of brown sugar and ¼ cup of soda.
5. Dip the chicken wings into the mixture and then put them in a broiler for about 2 minutes.
6. Serve and enjoy!!!

Jalapeno Hot Popper and Chicken Dip

Preparation Time: 3 minutes

Cook Time: 12 minutes

Total Time: 15 minutes

Serves: 10

Calories: 309 kcal

Ingredient:

- 1 Lb. boneless chicken breast

- 3/4 Cup of sour cream

- ½ Cup of panko bread crumbs

- 8 Oz .cream cheese

- 3 Jalapenos sliced

- 8 Oz. cheddar cheese

- ½ Cup of water

Cooking Instructions:

1. Put the sliced Jalapenos, chicken breast, cream cheese and water into your Ninja Foodi.
2. Cook in your Ninja Foodi on high pressure for about 12 minutes. When the cooking time is up, do quick release and shred chicken using fork.
3. Put 6 Oz. cheddar cheese and sour cream. Keep them on a baking pan and pour the remaining cheese and panko bread crumbs.
4. Put in the broiler for about 3 minutes.
5. Serve and enjoy!!!

Crack Chicken

Preparation Time: 5 minutes

Cook Time: 15 minutes

Total Time: 20 minutes

Serves: 4

Calories: 165 kcal

Ingredient:

- 8 Slices cooked bacon

- ½ Cup of water

- 1 Cup cheddar cheese

- 2 Boneless chicken breast

- 1 Packet ranch seasoning

- 8 Oz. cream cheese

Cooking Instructions:

1. Put cream cheese and chicken in your Ninja Foodi.
2. Pour in the packet of ranch seasoning on the top and put ½ cup of water.
3. Cook on your Ninja Foodi on high pressure for about 15 minutes. When the cooking time is up, do a quick release.
4. Get the chicken out and use fork to shred the chicken. Reduce the temperature of your Ninja Foodi to low.
5. Add the chicken back again. Put bacon. Give it a good stir.
6. Serve and enjoy!!!

Cracked up Tator Tots with Ranch Chicken

Preparation Time: 2 minutes

Cook Time: 20 minutes

Total Time: 22 minutes

Serves: 4

Ingredient:

- 2 Chicken breasts

- 1 Packet ranch seasoning

- 1 Cup of water

- 1 Bag of frozen tater tots

- 16 Oz. cheddar cheese

- 6 Slices of cooked bacon

Cooking Instructions:

1. Preheat oven to 350. Cook your tater tots.
2. Put the chicken breast in your Ninja Foodi, put a cup of water and ranch season packet.
3. Cook on your Ninja Foodi on high pressure for about 12 minutes. When the cooking time is up, do a quick release.
4. Get the chicken breast out from Ninja Foodi and shred with 2 forks. Combine together tatertots, together chicken.
5. Pour cheese on top and bacon. Bake for about 5 minutes.
6. Serve and enjoy!!!

Beer Can Chicken

Preparation Time: 2 minutes

Cook Time: 30 minutes

Total Time: 32 minutes

Serves: 10

Calories: 899 Kcal.

Ingredients:

- 6 Lbs. whole chicken

- 1 Tsp. paprika

- 1 Tsp. celery salt

- 1 Tsp. garlic powder

- 1 16 Oz. can of beer

- 1 Onion

- 2 Stalks of celery

- 1 Cup of water

- 4 Tbsp. butter

- 1 Tsp. salt

Cooking Instructions:

1. Wash and rinse your chicken, pat dry and put butter under the skin. Brush seasons on the chicken.
2. Slice your veggies into large chunks, put in the pot and then add 1 cup water. Open the can of beer.
3. Add the chicken in such a way that the chicken will be standing on the beer. Put the chicken into your Ninja Foodi on top of the beer.
4. Cook on your Ninja Foodi on high pressure for about 30 minutes. When the cooking time is up, do a quick release for about 20 minutes.
5. Serve and enjoy!!!

Fall off the Bone Ribs

Preparation Time: 5 minutes

Cook Time: 27 minutes

Total Time: 32 minutes

Serves: 2

Ingredients:

- 1 Coors Light Beer

- 1 Cup of BBQ Sauce

- 2 Racks of ribs

- 2 Cups apple juice

Cooking Instructions:

1. Set your Ninja Foodi to sauté mode, put beer and apple juice.
2. Put the ribs into the pot by placing the meat side down.
3. Close the lid and cook on your Ninja Foodi using meat/stew mode for about 30 minutes.
4. When the cooking time is up, do a quick release for about 10 minutes. Get the ribs out from the Ninja Foodi.
5. Add the BBQ sauce on top of the ribs. Put the ribs in your broiler for about 2 minutes on each side.
6. Serve and enjoy!!!

BEEF & PORK RECIPES

Pizza Bagels

Preparation Time: 10 minutes

Cook Time: 6 minutes

Total Time: 16 minutes

Serves: 2

Ingredients:

- 6 Slices pepperoni, divided

- ½ Cup of shredded mozzarella cheese, divided

- 1 Bagel, divided in half

- ¼ Cup of pizza sauce, divided

Cooking Instructions:

1. Put the Ninja Foodi rack in the pot, lock the crisping lid and preheat the Ninja Foodi for about 3 minutes.
2. Put bagel halves on the rack. Lock the crisping lid. Press Broil and select to cook for about to 3 minutes.
3. Immediately the cooking time is up, pour 2 Tbsp. pizza sauce on each bagel half. Spray with cheese.
4. Top with 3 pepperoni slices apiece and sprinkle with cheese. Lock the crisping lid Close lid, press Broil.
5. Select to cook for about to 3 minutes. Get the pizza out from the rack and allow it to cool for sometimes.
6. Serve and enjoy!!!

Parmesan Pork Chops

Preparation Time: 10 minutes

Cook Time: 8 minutes

Total Time: 18 minutes

Serves: 2

Ingredients:

- 2 Eggs

- Olive oil

- 2 Lbs. boneless pork chops

- ½ Cup grated parmesan cheese

- 1 Tbsp. Italian seasoning

- 1 Cup of Italian style bread crumbs

Cooking Instructions:

1. Press stovetop high on your Ninja Foodi. Put olive oil into Ninja Foodi so that a thin layer would be formed.
2. In a medium mixing bowl, beat the eggs and pour in the bowl. In a Ziploc bag, put the bread crumbs, seasonings and grated cheese.
3. Lock the bag and shake it thoroughly. Coat the pork chop in the egg mixture, put inside the baggie and shake it carefully.
4. Put the pork chops in your Ninja Foodi, lock the lid and cook for about 8 minutes on each side.
5. Serve and enjoy!!!

Bacon Ranch Beef Stroganoff

Preparation Time: 10 minutes

Cook Time: 8 minutes

Total Time: 18 minutes

Serves: 4

Ingredients:

- 1 ½ Lbs. ground beef

- 1 Lb. egg noodles

- 6 Cups of beef broth

- 3/4 Cup of real crumbled bacon

- 16 Oz. sour cream

- 2 Packets ranch dressing mixture

- 2 Tsp. garlic powder

Cooking Instructions:

1. Set your Ninja Foodi to sauté mode. Put the ground beef, garlic powder and sauté. Put the noodles and use broth to the noodles.
2. Cook on your Ninja Foodi on high pressure for about 8 minutes. When the cooking time is up, do a quick release for about 10 minutes.
3. Put the sour cream, bacon and ranch mixture into the noodles and give it a good stir.
4. Serve and enjoy!!!

Pork Tenderloin and Green Beans

Preparation Time: 10 minutes

Cook Time: 10 minutes

Total Time: 20 minutes

Serves: 4

Ingredients:

- 1 Lb. frozen green beans

- 1 ½ cups of water

- 1.15 Lb. pork tenderloin

Cooking Instructions:

1. Put water in your Ninja Foodi and put the tenderloin.
2. Place the green beans on top of the meat. Cook on your Ninja Foodi on high pressure for about 8 minutes.
3. When the cooking time is up, do a natural pressure release for about 15 minutes.
4. Serve and enjoy!!!

Pasta with Ground Beef

Preparation Time: 10 minutes

Cook Time: 10 minutes

Total Time: 20 minutes

Serves: 4

Ingredients:

- 1 Lb. ground beef

- 1 Tsp. minced garlic

- 12 Oz. box gluten-free pasta

- 1x 28 oz. can crushed tomatoes

Cooking Instructions:

1. Set your Ninja Foodi to sauté mode. Put Place the ground beef into the Ninja Foodi cooking pan on a medium heat pan.
2. Sauté over medium heat. Remove the beef and keep aside. Add the gluten-free pasta in the Ninja Foodi cooking pan.
3. Pour in the crushed tomatoes, minced garlic and the water into the Ninja Foodi. Give it a good stir.
4. Lock the lid and cook on a medium heat for about 15 minutes. Stir continuously while cooking.
5. Switch off the heat on the pan and spray in the shredded mozzarella.
6. Serve and enjoy!!!

Italian Beef and Rice

Preparation Time: 10 minutes

Cook Time: 35 minutes

Total Time: 45 minutes

Serves: 4

Ingredients:

- 1 ½ Cups of white rice

- 16 Oz. frozen mixed vegetables

- 1 Tbsp. Italian seasoning

- 1 ½ Lbs. ground beef

- 4 Oz. shredded mozzarella cheese

- 2x 14 ½ Oz. cans diced tomatoes

- 1 14 ½ Oz. can water

Cooking Instructions:

1. Place your Ninja Foodi on stovetop high settings. Put the ground beef and sauté. Immediately the meat is browned, switch the Ninja foodi to dry oven 350°F.
2. Put rice, mixed vegetables, diced tomatoes and water. Lock the lid and cook for about 20 minutes.
3. Immediately the cooking time is up, open the lid and stir. Pour the shredded cheese on the top.
4. Serve and enjoy!!!

Lasagna Shells with Meat Sauce

Preparation Time: 10 minutes

Cook Time: 5 minutes

Total Time: 15 minutes

Serve: 4

Ingredients:

- 1 Lbs. ground beef

- ¾ Lbs. sweet Italian sausage

- 1 Lb. large pasta shells

- 2x 28 Oz. cans tomato sauce

- 2 Tbsp. Italian seasoning

- 3.5 Cups of water

- 8 Oz. ricotta cheese

- 2 Cups of shredded mozzarella cheese

Cooking Instructions:

1. Set the Ninja Foodi on sauté mode. Place the ground beef and the sausage into the Ninja Foodie. Cook the meat to become brown.
2. Once the meat is browned, take away the sausage and slice them, then return them to the Ninja Foodi. Put in the pasta into the Ninja Foodi.
3. Empty the tomato sauce on top of the pasta then put the seasoning and water. Mix the combination and make sure all of the pasta is covered. Cover the Ninja Foodi.
4. Set the Ninja Foodi to cook for about 5 minutes. Open the Ninja Foodi and add the ricotta to the pot and mix well.
5. Put the shredded mozzarella to the pot and mix well.
6. Serve and enjoy!!!

Bacon Ranch Beef Stroganoff

Preparation Time: 10 minutes

Cook Time: 8 minutes

Total Time: 18 minutes

Serve: 4

Ingredients:

- 16 Oz. sour cream

- 2 Packets ranch dressing mix

- 2 Tsp. garlic powder

- 1.5 Lbs. ground beef

- 1 Lb. egg noodles

- 6 Cups beef broth

- ¾ Cup real crumbled bacon

- Shredded cheddar cheese

Cooking Instructions:

1. Set the Ninja Foodi to sauté mode. Put the ground beef, garlic powder and brown the meat into the Ninja Foodi.
2. Put the noodles and beef broth to the Ninja Foodie. Set the Ninja Foodi to cook for about 8 minutes.
3. When done, open and add the bacon, sour cream and ranch mix to the noodles and combine. Garnish with shredded cheddar.
4. Serve and enjoy

Italian Beef & Rice

Preparation Time: 10 minutes

Cook Time: 10 minutes

Total Time: 20 minutes

Serves: 4

Ingredients:

- 2 Tsp. garlic powder

- 2 Tsp. onion powder

- 1x 28 Oz. can diced tomatoes seasoned with basil, garlic and oregano

- 1.5 Lbs. ground beef

- 2 Cups of white rice

- 16 Oz. frozen mixed vegetables

- 1 Tbsp. Italian seasoning

- 2 Cups of water

Cooking Instructions:

1. Set the Ninja Foodi to sauté mode. Put the ground beef into the Ninja Foodi and then cook it.
2. When the meat has finished cooking, put the rice, seasonings, water, vegetables and tomatoes.
3. Cover the lid of the Ninja Foodi and seal. Set the Ninja Foodie to cook for about 8 minutes. Top with shredded mozzarella cheese as garnish.
4. Serve and enjoy!!!

One-Pot Baked Ziti

Preparation Time: 10 minutes

Cook Time: 15 minutes

Total Time: 25 minutes

Serves: 4

Ingredients:

- 1 Lb. ground beef

- 8 Oz. fresh mozzarella

- 2 Tbsp. olive oil

- System minced onion

- 1 Lb. ziti

- 1 26 Oz. jar pasta sauce

- 2 Cups of water

- 8 Oz. ricotta cheese

Cooking Instructions:

1. On a stovetop high setting, preheat your Ninja Foodi for about 5 minutes. Put olive oil, ground beef and onion into the Ninja Foodi pot.
2. Sauté the ground beef for about 8 minutes. Put the ziti, pasta sauce and water to the Ninja Foodi. Give it a good stir.
3. Keep the Ninja Foodi on Auto-iQ Layered Bowls Recipe 4 setting and push the start button. When the cooking time is up, open the lid.
4. Set the oven to 350°F. Put the ricotta cheese and give it a good stir. Put the slices of the fresh mozzarella on top of the pasta.
5. Lock the lid and cook for about 15 minutes.
6. Serve and enjoy!!!

FISH & SEAFOODS

Apricot and Country Mustard Salmon

Preparation Time: 5 minutes

Cook Time: 10 minutes

Total Time: 15 minutes

Serves: 4

Ingredients:

- 2 Cups of water

- 1½ Lbs. salmon fillets

- Salt

- ¼ Cup of apricot preserves

- 2 Tbsp. country

- Dijon-style mustard

- Ground black pepper

Cooking Instruction:

1. Pour preserves and mustard in a small mixing bowl. Pour 2 cups of water into the Ninja Foodi.
2. Put salt and black pepper. Put the fish on roasting rack. Pour the preserve mixture on fish and put it into the Ninja Foodi.
3. Cook at 400°F for 20 minutes.
4. Serve and enjoy!!!

Cod with Tomato Caper Sauce & Sugar Peas

Preparation Time: 5 minutes

Cook Time: 20 minutes

Total Time: 25 minutes

Serves: 4

Ingredients:

- 4 Cod fillets

- ¾ Lb. sugar snap peas

- 2 Medium tomatoes, chopped

- 2 Cloves garlic, minced

- 1 Tbsp. chopped fresh basil leaves

- ½ Tsp. salt

- ½ Cup of white wine

- 2 Tbsp. drained capers

Cooking Instructions:

1. Put wine, capers, garlic, tomatoes, basil, and salt into your Ninja Foodi.
2. Put fish and keep snap peas on top of the fish.
3. Set Oven to 375°F. Lock the lid and cook for 10 minutes.
4. Serve and enjoy!!!

Fish Packets

Preparation Time: 5 minutes

Cook Time: 30 minutes

Total Time: 35 minutes

Serves: 4

Ingredients:

- 4 Tbsp. of margarine

- 2 Packets of Knorr chicken flavored rice

- 2 Fish packets

- 16 Oz. package of frozen Asian stir fry vegetables

- 4 Cups of water

Cooking Instructions:

1. Set the Ninja Foodi to stovetop high, melt all your margarine, put the stir fry vegetables, chicken flavored rice and water.
2. Fold the fish in foil and put them on top of the mixture. This will enable the fish to be steamed when the rice and vegetables are still cooking.
3. Set your Ninja Foodi on Oven setting. Set to cook at 300°F for 30 minutes. Close the lid and press start button.
4. Serve and enjoy!!!

Garlic Parmesan Shrimp with Angel Hair Pasta and Broccoli

Preparation Time: 5 minutes

Cook Time: 18 minutes

Total Time: 23 minutes

Serves: 2

Ingredients:

- Red pepper flakes

- 1 Bag of frozen

- 3 Cups water

- 1 Box angel hair pasta

- 2 Jars of Ragu Parmesan Garlic Sauce

- 1 Bag frozen chopped broccoli

Cooking Instructions:

1. Except the shrimp, mix together all ingredients and pour them into your Ninja Foodi.
2. On oven settings, cook at 325°F for about 15 minutes.
3. After the 15 minutes, put a bag of frozen, already cooked shrimp and cook again for about 3 minutes.
4. Serve and enjoy!!!

Papi's Pepper Garlic Shrimp

Preparation Time: 5 minutes

Cook Time: 7 minutes

Total Time: 12 minutes

Serves: 2

Ingredients:

- Butter

- 1½ Lbs. of shrimp

- 2 Handfuls of cherry tomatoes

- 6 Tbsp. olive oil

- 5 Heaping tablespoons black pepper

- 4 Cubes of frozen garlic cubes

- 1 Tbsp. onion powder

Cooking Instructions:

1. Melt your butter in your Ninja Foodi and put all the ingredients except shrimp and tomatoes. Mix thoroughly.
2. Set your Ninja Foodi to Stovetop High. Cook for about 1 minute put shrimp and cook for 3 minutes again.
3. When 3 minutes is up, flip the shrimp over. Put tomatoes and cook for another 3 minutes.
4. Serve and enjoy!!!

Salmon Filet Spinach Salad Bake

Preparation Time: 10 minutes

Cook Time: 30 minutes

Total Time: 12 minutes

Serves: 2

Ingredients:

- Salmon filet

- Fresh spinach

- Salt

- Pepper

- 8 Oz. box mushrooms, sliced

- 1 Box grape tomatoes, cut in half

- granulated garlic

- French dressing

Cooking Instruments:

1. In a small mixing bowl, combine together tomatoes, salt, pepper, garlic, mushrooms and dressing.
2. Put your salmon in the Ninja Foodi cooking pan. Spread the mixture on top of the salmon and put 2 cups of water into your Ninja Foodi.
3. Keep your rack and the pan on the top. Set your Ninja Foodi to Oven setting and set to cook at 375°F for 30 minutes.
4. Serve and enjoy!!!

Salmon Filets and Quinoa

Preparation Time: 10 minutes

Cook Time: 22 minutes

Total Time: 32 minutes

Serves: 3

Ingredients:

- 1 Cup rinsed quinoa

- 1 Cup rinsed mushrooms

- 2 Salmon filets

- 1 Cup chard wine

- 1 Cup chicken broth

Cooking Instructions:

1. Select Oven setting on your Ninja Foodi at 350°F. Put broth, quinoa, wine and mushrooms. Mix properly.
2. Season your salmon on rack and keep the rack on top of the broth mixture. Cook on your Ninja Foodi for about 15 minutes.
3. After 15 minutes, remove salmon and keep aside. Cook the quinoa for another 7 minutes. Top with salad.
4. Serve and enjoy!!!

Salmon Patties

Preparation Time: 10 minutes

Cook Time: 22 minutes

Total Time: 32 minutes

Serves: 1

Ingredients:

- 1 Egg

- 2/3 Cup bread crumbs

- Salt

- 2 Small cans salmon, drained

- Pepper

Cooking Instructions:

1. Combine together and prepare 4 patties.
2. On a stovetop high, put 1 Tbsp. oil in the Ninja Foodi and brown both sides of the patties. Top with salad.
3. Serve and enjoy!!!

Seafood Italiano with Pasta

Preparation Time: 10 minutes

Cook Time: 22 minutes

Total Time: 32 minutes

Serves: 1

Ingredients:

- 1 Lb. shrimp

- ½ Cup of red wine

- 20 Oz. package frozen ravioli

- 1 Lb. Patagonian scallops

- 1 Clove crushed garlic

- 2- 24 Oz. jars quality pasta sauce

- 2 Tbs. olive oil

Cooking Instructions:

1. Set the Ninja Foodi to Stovetop high and prepare your ingredients.
2. Put oil and sear the scallops, shrimp and garlic. Put the pasta sauce and wine. Give it a good mix and put the ravioli.
3. Pour them into the sauce and set Ninja Foodi to Stovetop Low for 30 minutes. Stir continuously.
4. Serve and enjoy!!!

Shrimp and Crab Boil

Preparation Time: 10 minutes

Cook Time: 45 minutes

Total Time: 55 minutes

Serves: 4

Ingredients:

- 2 Bay leaves

- Garlic cloves

- 4 Cups of water

- 1 Quartered onion

- 2 Lemon halves

- Creole seasoning

- McCormick crab and shrimp boil seasoning bag

- 2 Tbsp. Zatarain's concentrated boil

Cooking Instructions:

1. Except the Creole seasoning, put all the ingredients into the Ninja Foodi.
2. Set your Ninja Foodi to Stovetop High.
3. Steam cook for 45 minutes. Top with Creole seasoning.
4. Serve and enjoy!!!

SOUP RECIPES

Turkey Minestrone Soup

Preparation Time: 15 minutes

Cook Time: 47 minutes

Total Time: 1 hour 2 minutes

Serves: 4

Ingredients:

- 2 Tsp. extra virgin olive oil

- Pepper

- 1 Lb. uncooked lean ground turkey

- 1 Onion, peeled and chopped

- ½ Box (8 Oz.) uncooked ditalini pasta

- 6 Cups of chicken stock

- 4 Carrots, peeled and chopped

- ½ Head green cabbage, chopped

- 1 Can (15 Oz.)

- Diced tomatoes

- 1 Cup of water

- Salt

- 3 Cloves garlic, peeled and chopped

- 3 Stalks celery, chopped

Cooking Instructions:

1. Preheat the pot for about 5 minutes. Put oil into the pot and heat for about 2 minutes.
2. Put onion, garlic, turkey, celery, and carrots. Cook for about 15 minutes. Keep stirring it while cooking.
3. Put tomatoes, water, cabbage, pasta, stock, salt, and pepper into the pot. Stir thoroughly to mix properly and close the pot.
4. Serve and enjoy!!!

French Onion Soup with Crispy Grilled Cheese Croutons

Preparation Time: 5 minutes

Cook Time: 35 minutes

Total Time: 40 minutes

Serves: 4

Ingredients:

Soup:

- 1 Tbsp. olive oil

- 1 Tbsp. balsamic vinegar

- Salt

- 4 Medium yellow onions, thinly sliced

- 4 Cloves of garlic, minced

- 1 Tbsp. tamari

- Black pepper

- 6 Cups of vegetable broth

- 1 Tbsp. vegan Worcestershire

Grilled Cheese Croutons:

- 4 Slices of bread

- 1 Tbsp. olive oil

- 2 Slices vegan cheddar

Cooking Instructions:

1. Preheat your cooker for about 5 minutes. Put the onions, garlic and olive oil into the pot and sauté for 10 minutes.

2. Put the Worcestershire sauce, vegetable broth, balsamic vinegar, tamari, salt and pepper. Close the lid and be sure the pressure release valve is in the SEAL position.
3. Select High Pressure and set the cooking time to 15 minutes. Press Start/Stop button. Make the grilled cheese croutons while the soup is cooking.
4. Gather 2 sandwiches with the bread and cheese. Rub olive oil on the tops of the sandwiches. Cut the sandwiches into cubes of 1-inch and keep aside.
5. Immediately the cooking time is up, do quick pressure release and thereafter remove the lid.
6. Place the croutons on top of the soup. Lock the lid and cook for 14 minutes.
7. Serve and enjoy!!!

Taiwanese Beef Noodle Soup

Preparation Time: 15 minutes

Cook Time: 30 minutes

Total Time: 45 minutes

Serves: 4

Calories: 590

Ingredients:

- 2 ½ Lbs. bone-in beef shank

- 1 Large onion, quartered

- ½ Cup of soy sauce

- ¼ Cup of Shaoxing wine

- 2 Tomatoes, quartered

- 4 Peeled garlic cloves

- 1 Piece of large ginger, sliced

- 3 Star anise

- 2 Lbs. Asian noodles

- Green onions

- 2 Cinnamon sticks

- 1/2 Tsp. fennel seed

- 1/2 Tsp. ground clove

- 1/2 Tsp. ground cumin

Cooking Instructions:

1. Put water into a large pot and boil. Dip the beef shanks into the water for about 3 minutes. Get the beef shanks out.
2. Put the beef shanks into the Ninja Foodi and then pour in the remaining ingredients. Do not put water. During cooking period, the beef brings out water.
3. Cook the beef using Meat Preset for about 26 minutes. Cook the noodles and share them equally bowls.
4. Top the noodles with meat and soup.
5. Serve and enjoy!!!

French Onion Soup Chicken Bake

Preparation Time: 10 minutes

Cook Time: 23 minutes

Total Time: 33 minutes

Serves: 4

Ingredients:

- 1.5 Lbs. Chicken breast

- 2 Medium Onions

- 2 Tbsp. Garlic Minced

- 3 Tbsp. olive oil

- 11 Slices Swiss

- Black Pepper

- 10 ½ Oz. can French onion soup with beef stock

Cooking Instructions:

1. Put 1½ Tbsp. oil and sliced onions into the Ninja Foodi. Sauté for about 3 minutes, remove and keep aside.
2. Clean the bottom of the Ninja Foodi pot and put 1½ Tbsp. oil. Season both sides of the chicken with pepper.
3. Put minced garlic to the pot and then place chicken breasts on top. Sauté both sides of the chicken for about 2 minutes.
4. Place the cooked onions on top of chicken breast. Put 1 can of soup and 1 can of water. Press Manual Pressure and set to cook for 20 minutes.
5. Immediately the cooking time is up, do quick pressure release for about 10 minutes and thereafter remove the lid.
6. Put cheese slices on top. Set the Ninja Foodi to 375°F and bake for 3 minutes. Top with salad and veggie.
7. Serve and enjoy!!!

Sausage Soup

Preparation Time: 15 minutes

Cook Time: 10 minutes

Total Time: 25 minutes

Serves: 6

Calories: 431kcal

Ingredients:

- 1 Lb. sausage roll

- ½ Onion diced

- 16 Oz. Northern beans dry

- ¼ Tsp. salt

- ½ Cup of parmesan cheese

- 6 Cup of water

- 1 Tbsp. garlic minced

- 4 Cup of chicken broth

- 28 Oz. crushed tomatoes

- 1 Tsp. oregano dried

Cooking Instructions:

1. Put the beans into your Ninja Foodi with 6 cups of water. Set Ninja Foodi to bean mode for 60 minutes.
2. When the cooking time is up, do a quick release, drain and keep aside. Press Sauté button on your Ninja Foodi and put a little olive oil, sausage and diced onion.
3. Cook to ensure does not have pink look. Put the spices, onions and meat. Mix properly. Put cooked beans, crushed tomatoes and chicken broth.
4. Give it a good stir. Trim out the stem on fresh kale and slice them into small chunks. Put them into Ninja Foodi.
5. Close lid Set Ninja Foodi to Manual High Pressure to cook for 10 minutes.

6. Immediately the cooking time is up, do quick pressure release for about 10 minutes and remove the lid.
7. Serve and enjoy!!!

Bean Soup

Preparation Time: 15 minutes

Cook Time: 40 minutes

Total Time: 55 minutes

Serves: 6

Calories: 147kcal

Ingredients:

- 2 Stalks celery, diced

- 2 Green onions, diced

- 32 Oz. chicken broth

- 2 Tbsp. olive oil

- 5 Strips bacon, diced

- 1 ½ Cup of beans dry

- 1 Cup of onion, diced

Cooking Instructions:

1. Add your beans into Ninja Foodi and pour in 4 cups of water. Lock lid and steam valve. Cook on bean setting for 35 minutes.
2. Immediately the cooking time is up, do Natural Pressure release for about 10 minutes and thereafter remove the lid.
3. Drain the beans and keep aside. Set the Ninja Foodi to sauté mode. Put diced onion, olive oil and bacon.
4. Cook for about 5 minutes. Switch off the Ninja Foodi. Put all the remaining ingredients alongside with the cooked beans.
5. Give it a good stir. Lock the lid and steam valve. Press Soup mode and set to cook for 10 minutes.
6. Do a quick release and top with grated parmesan cheese.
7. Serve and enjoy!!!

Potato Cheese Soup

Preparation Time: 15 minutes

Cook Time: 8 minutes

Total Time: 23 minutes

Serves: 5

Calories 490kcal

Ingredients:

- 1/4 Onion diced

- 1 Tsp. salt

- 1 Tsp. garlic powder

- 1.5 C cheddar cheese, shredded

- 1 Cup of heavy cream

- 1 Tbsp. chives for garnish

- 1 Cup of celery diced

- 6 Potatoes diced small, skins removed

- 6 Cup of chicken broth

Cooking Instructions:

1. Put potatoes, celery, onion, salt, carrot, garlic powder and broth into your Ninja Foodi and give it a good stir.
2. Close the lid and set the Ninja Foodi to cook for about 8 minutes. Immediately the cooking time is up, do Quick Pressure release for about 10 minutes.
3. Carefully remove the lid. Open the lid and give it a good stir. Put 1 ½ cup of cheese, and heavy cream.
4. Give everything a good mix and set aside. Flip onto a serving plate and garnish with extra cheese and parsley.
5. Serve and enjoy!!!

Split Pea soup

Preparation Time: 10 minutes

Cook Time: 8 hours

Total Time: 8 hours 10 minutes

Serves: 8

Calories: 288kcal

Ingredients:

- 16 Oz split peas dry

- ½ Tsp. salt

- 3 Cups of ham bite size-diced

- 7 Cups vegetable broth

- 2 Stalks celery diced

- 1/3 Onion diced

- 2 Carrots diced

Cooking Instructions:

1. Put vegetable broth and dried peas into your Ninja Foodi. Slice your veggies to medium sizes and put to Crockpot.
2. Put onion Dice onion and salt. Sprinkle your diced ham into your Ninja Foodi. Close and cook for about 8 hours on low heat.
3. Put more broth for more thinness. It will be thicker if you allow it to rest for sometimes.
4. Serve and enjoy!!!

Tomato Basil Soup

Preparation Time: 10 minutes

Cook Time: 9 minutes

Total Time: 19 minutes

Serves: 8

Calories: 271kcal

Ingredients:

- ½ Onion, diced

- 29 Oz. tomato sauce

- 8 Basil leaves fresh, or 1 tbsp. dried basil

- 2 Cup of tortellini optional

- 1 Tsp. pepper

- Salt

- 1 Tbsp. garlic, minced

- 1 Cup of heavy whipping cream

Cooking Instructions:

1. Press Sauté button on your Ninja Foodi and put a little olive oil, garlic and onions. Sauté for few minutes.
2. Switch off your Ninja Foodi and put half of basil leaves can of tomato sauce. Give it a good stir. Pres Manual High Pressure and set to cook for 2 minutes.
3. Immediately the cooking time is up, do Quick Pressure release for about 10 minutes and thereafter remove the lid.
4. Press Sauté button again on your Ninja Foodi. Put 2 cups of stuffed tortellini noodles. Sauté for about 5 minutes.
5. Stir occasionally. Put whipping cream and give it a good stir. Cook for another 2 minutes. Top with basil.
6. Serve and enjoy!!!

Corn Chowder

Preparation Time: 10 minutes

Cook Time: 20 minutes

Total Time: 30 minutes

Serves: 6

Calories: 292kcal

Ingredients:

- ½ Green pepper, diced

- 2 Cups of chicken broth

- 3 Strips bacon, cooked and diced

- 3/4 Cup of cheddar cheese, shredded

- 4 Potatoes, peeled and diced

- 1 Tsp. salt

- ¼ Tsp. pepper

- 3 Cups of corn kernels frozen

- 1 Small onion, diced

- 1 Cup of half and half

Cooking Instructions:

1. Put onion, green pepper, corn, chicken broth, potatoes, salt and pepper into your Ninja Foodi and heat on low for about 8 hours.
2. Immediately cooking time is up, put half and half. Close the lid and cook at high pressure for about 20 minutes.
3. Keep on stirring it while cooking. Top with shredded cheese and chopped bacon.
4. Serve and enjoy!!!

RICE & PASTA RECIPES

Caprese Pasta Salad

Preparation Time: 10 minutes

Cook Time: 12 minutes

Total Time: 22 minutes

Serves: 6

Ingredients:

- 8 Oz. bocconcini mozzarella

- ¼ Cup of chopped fresh parsley

- 12 Oz. dried orecchiette pasta

- 2/3 Cup of olive oil

- 5 Tbsp. red wine vinegar

- 1/3 Cup of chopped fresh basil

- ¼ Cup of chopped fresh chives

- ½ Tsp. kosher salt

- ½ Tsp. black pepper

- 2 Tbsp. capers, drained and chopped

- 3 Cloves garlic, minced

- 2 Cups of cherry tomatoes, halved

Cooking Instructions:

1. Put dressing ingredients in a large bowl and mix thoroughly. Remain about 2 Tbsp. of dressing and keep aside.
2. Put fresh mozzarella and cherry tomatoes into mixing bowl with the dressing and give it a good mix. Allow it to absorb for about 30 minutes.

3. Boil pasta, drain and put oil. Allow it to cool for about 5 minutes. Put pasta into mixing bowl and give it a good stir.
4. Flip onto a serving plate. Put in the refrigerator for about 24 hours. Top with reserved dressing.
5. Serve and enjoy!!!

Bacon Cheeseburger Pasta Bake

Preparation Time: 10 minutes

Cook Time: 30 minutes

Total Time: 40 minutes

Serves: 6

Ingredients:

- 1/3 Cup of chopped dill pickles

- 2 Tsp. Worcestershire sauce

- 2 Tsp. ground dry mustard

- 1 ½ Tsp. packed light brown sugar

- ½ Tsp. garlic powder

- ½ Tsp. kosher salt

- 6 Slices cooked and crumbled bacon

- 1/3 Cup of yellow onion, diced

- Minced fresh parsley

- 7 Slices of American cheese

- ½ Tsp. black pepper

- 3 Cups of water

- 15 Oz. can tomato sauce

- 1 Lb. lean ground beef

- 3 Cups of dried, uncooked elbow macaroni pasta

Cooking Instructions:

1. Preheat oven to 475° F. Put non-stick cooking spray on your baking pan. Keep aside.

2. Mix together the tomato sauce, pickles, water, Worcestershire sauce, garlic powder, dry mustard, brown sugar, salt and pepper on a large mixing bowl. Mix properly.
3. Crumble beef into small ½ inch pieces with your fingers and put dried macaroni. Put them to the mixture and mix properly.
4. Put the mixture into the baking pan. Close with aluminum foil and bake for 25 minutes.
5. Get the dish out from the oven, remove the aluminum foil. Give it a good stir.
6. Top with crumbled bacon and American cheese slices. Bake again uncovered for about 7 minutes.
7. Allow it to cool for about 10 minutes. Top with minced onion and chopped pickles.
8. Serve and enjoy!!!

Spaghetti Bolognese Sauce

Preparation Time: 10 minutes

Cook Time: 8 hours

Total Time: 8 hours 10 minutes

Serves: 8

Ingredients:

- 2 Tbsp. olive oil

- 1 Lb. ground beef

- 1 Lb. ground Italian sausage

- 1 Onion minced

- 2 Carrots, very finely chopped

- 8 Cloves garlic minced

- 14 Oz. cans crushed tomatoes

- 24 Oz. jar marinara sauce

- 1 Cup of water

- 3 Bay leaves

- 3 Tsp. better than chicken bouillon

- 3 Tsp. dried basil

- 2 Tsp. balsamic vinegar

- 2 Tsp. dried oregano

- 2 Tsp. sugar

- 2 Tsp. kosher salt

- 2 Tsp. dried parsley

- ½ Tsp. dried thyme

- 1 Tsp. black pepper

- ½ Tsp. crushed red pepper flakes

Cooking Instructions:

1. On a skillet, heat olive oil on a medium heat.
2. Put Italian sausage and ground beef. Cook for about 6 minutes. Stir and crumble both beef and sausage.
3. When 3 minutes remains on the cooking time, put carrot, garlic and onion to beef and cook.
4. Drain and get rid of excess grease. Put meat mixture into Ninja Foodi and put the reserved sauce ingredients.
5. Mix properly. Close and cook on low heat for about 8 hours.
6. Serve and enjoy!!!

Spanish rice

Preparation Time: 5 minutes

Cook Time: 12 minutes

Total Time: 17 minutes

Serves: 4

Ingredients:

- 1 Chopped green pepper chopped

- 1 Cup of uncooked long grain rice

- ½ Tsp. salt

- 1 Garlic clove, minced

- 1 Tbsp. chili powder

- 2 Cups of tomato

- 1 Lb. ground beef

- 1 Small onion chopped

Cooking Instructions:

1. Put the ground beef into your Ninja Foodi. Press sauté button on your Ninja Foodi and sauté the ground beef to brown. Drain excess oil.
2. Put the green pepper, garlic, onion and chili powder. Cook for about 5 minutes. Put the reserved ingredients. Mix properly.
3. Secure the lid. Select Manual Low Pressure and set to cook for 12 minutes.
4. When the cooking time is up, do a quick pressures release.
5. Serve and enjoy!!!

Quick Chicken and Rice

Preparation Time: 10 minutes

Cook Time: 33 minutes

Total Time: 43 minutes

Serves: 4

Ingredients:

- 2 Tbsp. extra-virgin olive oil

- 1/8 Tsp. cayenne pepper

- 1 Bag of frozen peas and carrots

- 1 Lb. mushrooms, cleaned, sliced

- 2 Cups of long grain brown rice

- ½ Cup of white wine

- 2 Tsp. granulated garlic

- 2 Tsp. onion powder

- 3 Sprigs of fresh thyme

- ½ Tsp. ground white pepper

- 2 Cups of chicken stock

- 1 3/4 Lbs. boneless, skinless chicken thighs

- 1 Tbsp. kosher salt

- 2 Tsp. smoked paprika

Cooking Instructions:

1. Press Saute mode, set to high and preheat for 5 minutes. Put oil and mushrooms to the Ninja Foodi and Sauté for 5 minutes.

2. Put the remaining ingredients except frozen peas and carrots and give it a good stir. Secure the lid.
3. Ensure that the pressure release valve is set to Seal position. Press Manual High Pressure and set to cook for 22 minutes.
4. Immediately cooking time is up, do a natural pressure release for about 10 minutes. Open the lid and Stir in the frozen vegetables.
5. Cook for about for 5 minutes. Serve and enjoy!!!

Skinny Benihana Fried Rice

Preparation Time: 10 minutes

Cook Time: 14 minutes

Total Time: 24 minutes

Serves: 3

Ingredients:

- 2 Cups brown rice

- Half a white onion

- 3 Cloves of garlic, minced

- 2 Cups of water

- ½ Cup of soy sauce

- 1 Cup of carrots, diced

- 4 Scallions, chopped

- 1 Tbsp. sesame seeds

- 2 Pieces of lean steak, cubed

- 4 Eggs, scrambled.

- 1 Tsp. garlic powder

- 1 Cup of peas

- 2 Tbsp. ghee, melted

Cooking Instructions:

1. Put carrots, peas, rice, onions, minced garlic, 1 tbsp. of the soy sauce and water into your Ninja Foodi.
2. Sauté for about 10 minutes. Put ghee, soy sauce, cubed steak, honey, lemon and garlic powder. Sauté for about 4 minutes.

3. Push the rice to be by the sides and make a hole in the center and put the egg in the hole. Close the lid.
4. Cook for 7 minutes. Keep on stirring it while cooking. Top with chopped scallions and sesame seeds.
5. Serve and enjoy!!!

One-Pot Taco Rice

Preparation Time: 10 minutes

Cook Time: 35 minutes

Total Time: 45 minutes

Serves: 3

Ingredients:

- Shredded taco cheese

- Sour cream

- 1 ½ Lbs ground beef

- 1 ½ Cups of white rice

- 2 Packets taco seasoning

- 2 (14 ½) Oz. cans diced tomatoes

- 16 Oz. frozen corn

- 1 (14 ½) Oz. can water

Cooking Instructions:

1. Put the ground beef into your Ninja Foodi and then Sauté the beef to become brown. Set the Ninja Foodi to dry oven at 350°F.
2. Put rice, corn, diced tomatoes, seasoning, and water. Close the lid and cook for 20 minutes. Open the lid and stir.
3. Close the lid again and cook for another 15 minutes. Top with shredded cheese and sour cream.
4. Serve and enjoy!!!

Italian Beef and Rice

Preparation Time: 10 minutes

Cook Time: 25 minutes

Total Time: 35 minutes

Serves: 4

Ingredients:

- 16 Oz. frozen mixed vegetables

- 1 (14 1/2) Oz. can water

- 1 Tbsp. Italian seasoning

- 1/2 Lbs. ground beef

- 1/2 Cups of white rice

- 4 Oz. shredded mozzarella cheese

- 2 (14 1/2) Oz. cans diced tomatoes seasoned with basil and garlic

Cooking Instructions:

1. Put the ground beef into your Ninja Foodi and then Sauté the beef to become brown. Set the Ninja Foodi to dry oven at 350°F.
2. Put rice, mixed vegetables, diced tomatoes and water. Close the lid and cook for 20 minutes. Open the lid and stir.
3. Close the lid again and cook for another 15 minutes. Spread shredded cheese on the top. Close the lid and allow the cheese to melt for sometimes.
4. Serve and enjoy!!!

Beefy Broccoli Rice

Preparation Time: 8 minutes

Cook Time: 10 minutes

Total Time: 18 minutes

Serves: 2

Ingredients:

- ½ Lbs. ground beef

- 1 Jar double cheddar pasta sauce

- 1 Tsp. onion powder

- Cups of water

- ½ Cups of white rice

- 12 Oz. frozen chopped broccoli

- 1 Tsp. garlic powder

Cooking Instructions:

1. Put the ground beef into your Ninja Foodi and then Sauté the beef to become brown. Put rice and water.
2. Press Manual High Pressure and set to cook for 7 minutes. Immediately the cooking time is up, do a quick pressure release.
3. Put pasta sauce, onion powder, garlic powder and broccoli. Press the Steam setting and set the time to cook for 3 minutes. Stir thoroughly.
4. Serve and enjoy!!!

Ham and Pineapple Rice

Preparation Time: 8 minutes

Cook Time: 9 minutes

Total Time: 17 minutes

Serves: 2

Ingredients:

- 2 Tsp of garlic powder

- 1/3 Cup of teriyaki sauce

- 16 Oz cooked honey ham, diced

- 2 Cups of chicken broth

- 1 Cup of frozen peas and carrots

- 2 Tsp onion powder

- ½ Cups of uncooked rice

Cooking Instructions:

1. Put the chicken broth, rice, teriyaki sauce, garlic powder, onion powder, and vegetables into your Ninja Foodi. And give it a good stir.
2. Put the pineapple and give it a good stir. Press Manual Low Pressure on your Ninja Foodi and set to cook for about 9 minutes.
3. Immediately the cooking time is up, do a natural pressure release. Open the lid and give it a good stir.
4. Serve and enjoy!!!

BEAN & GRAIN RECIPES

Black Beans Chili

Preparation Time: 10 minutes

Cook Time: 20 minutes

Total Time: 30 minutes

Serves: 4

Ingredients:

- 2 Tbsp. chili powder

- 1 ½ Tsp. salt

- 3 Cloves garlic

- 3 Jalapenos, stemmed

- 1 ½ Tbsp. ground cumin

- 1 28 Oz. can crushed tomatoes

- 1Lb. extra lean ground beef

- 1 Medium onion, chopped

- 1 Large green pepper, chopped

- 2 Cans black beans

- Fresh stemmed and chopped cilantro

- 2 Canned chipotles plus 1 tablespoon adobo sauce

Cooking Instructions:

1. Put onion, pepper, garlic, meat and jalapenos into your Ninja Foodi. Keep the Ninja Foodi on Stovetop High settings.
2. Cook for about 20 minutes uncovered. Stir through on the cook time. Put in the ingredients that remained except cilantro.

3. Set the Ninja Foodi to Slow Cook High for about 3 hours. Top with cilantro.
4. Serve and enjoy!!!

White Bean Chicken Chili

Preparation Time: 10 minutes

Cook Time: 10 minutes

Total Time: 20 minutes

Serves: 4

Ingredients:

- 1 Whole Onion, chopped

- ½ Tsp. Chili Powder

- ½ Tsp. Black Pepper

- 1/8 Tsp. Ground Red Pepper

- 2 Tsp. Garlic

- 4 Cans Cannellini Beans

- 2 Cans Fat Free Reduced Sodium Chicken

- 1 Can Chopped Green Chile Peppers

- ½ Tsp. Chili Powder

- ½ Tsp. Black Pepper

- 1/8 Tsp. Ground Red Pepper

- 1 Tsp. Cumin

- 1 Tsp. Salt

- 3/4 Tsp. Dried Oregano

- 1 ½ Cups of Corn

- ½ Tsp. Chili Powder

- ½ Tsp. Black Pepper

- ¹/8 Tsp. Ground Red Pepper

Cooking Instructions:

1. Put olive oil, the ground chicken, garlic, salt, pepper, ground red pepper, oregano, chili powder, peppers and cumin.
2. Stir properly and Sauté for about 10 minutes. When it is almost cooked, put chicken broth, corn and green Chile pepper.
3. When cooking time is up, do a quick pressure release.
4. Serve and enjoy!!!

Cajun Ranch Corn Chips

Preparation Time: 10 minutes

Cook Time: 2 hours

Total Time: 2 hours 10 minutes

Serves: 1

Ingredients:

- 1 9.75 Oz. bag corn chips

- 1 Tbsp. Cajun spice

- ½ Cup of unsalted butter, melted

- 1 1.0 Oz. packet ranch dip mix

Cooking Instructions:

1. Spray nonstick cooking spray into your Ninja Foodi and put a bag of corn chips.
2. Melt butter and put it in a small mixing bowl with ranch seasoning and Cajun spice. Mix properly.
3. Pour the butter mixture into the Ninja Foodi. Give it a good stir. Select High Pressure on the Ninja Foodi to cook for about 2 hours.
4. Cook uncovered and keep stirring while cooking. Place a cookie sheet with wax paper.
5. When then cooking time is up, put the corn chips on the cookie sheet for it to cool.
6. Serve and enjoy!!!

Tuscan Garlicky Bean Soup

Preparation Time: 1 hour

Cook Time: 9 hours 2 minutes

Total Time: 10 hours 2 minutes

Serves: 2

Ingredients:

- 2 Cups dry Great Northern

- 3 Tbsp. olive oil

- 1 Tsp. salt

- ½ Tsp. black pepper

- 2 Garlic cloves

- 4 Tbsp. chopped parsley

- 1 Cup of water

- 1 Fat-free, low sodium chicken broth

Cooking Instructions:

1. Boil the beans in a large pot for about 2 minutes. Remove from heat. Close the pot and keep it for 1 hour.
2. Drain and pour out the water. Mix together beans, chicken and water in the Ninja Foodi.
3. In a skillet, Sauté parsley and garlic, salt and pepper. Close and cook on Low pressure for 9 hours.
4. Serve and enjoy!!!

Baked Kidney Beans

Preparation Time: 10 minutes

Cook Time: 5 hours

Total Time: 5 hours 10 minutes

Serves: 4

Ingredients:

- 2 Tbsp. bacon fat

- 1 Small onion

- 2 Cups raw kidney beans

- ¼ Cup molasses

- ½ Tsp. salt

- 1 Tsp. dry mustard

- ½ Cup sugar

Cooking Instructions:

1. Put beans in your pot and boil for 1 hour.
2. Put alongside with other ingredients in a small roaster.
3. Bake at 340°F for about 4 hours. Do not cover the beans with water.
4. Serve and enjoy!!!

Chicken with Black Beans and Sweet Potato

Preparation Time: 15 minutes

Cook Time: 8 hours

Total Time: 8 hours 15 minutes

Serves: 4

Ingredients:

- 1 Can 19 Oz. black beans

- 4 Medium sweet potatoes

- 8 Boneless, skinless chicken thighs

- 2 Tsp. ground cumin

- Pinch salt and pepper

- 1 Cup of chicken broth

- ½ Cup salsa

- 3 Garlic cloves, chopped

- 1 Tsp. ground paprika

- ½ Tsp. ground allspice

Cooking Instructions:

1. Except the chicken, beans and sweet potatoes mix together all the ingredients in a small mixing bowl.
2. Mix together the beans and sweet potatoes in your Ninja Foodi. Keep the chicken on top of the mixture and then pour broth mixture on the chicken.
3. Cook on low pressure for about 8 hours.
4. Serve and enjoy!!!

Chicken with White Beans

Preparation Time: 15 minutes

Cook Time: 4 hours

Total Time: 4 hours 15 minutes

Serves: 4

Ingredients:

- 2 Carrots, sliced

- 1 Cup of water

- Salt and pepper

- 1 Stalk celery, sliced

- 1 Small onion, diced

- 2 Cans (15 ½ Oz. each) Great Northern beans

- ½ Cup of low cal Italian salad dressing

- 4 Oz. boneless, skinless chicken breast tenders

Cooking Instructions:

1. Put onion, carrots, beans, celery into your Ninja Foodi and place chicken on top of bean mixture.
2. Put the salad dressing, salt and pepper with 1 cup water.
3. Close the lid and cook on low pressure 4 hours.
4. Serve and enjoy!!!

Black Bean Chicken

Preparation Time: 15 minutes

Cook Time: 10 hours

Total Time: 10 hours 15 minutes

Serves: 4

Ingredients:

- ½ Cup brown rice (uncooked)

- 1 Lb. boneless, skinless chicken breasts

- 2 Cans black beans

- 16 Oz. jarred salsa

Cooking Instructions:

1. Put chicken breasts into your Ninja Foodi.
2. Place rice, beans and salsa on top of the chicken.
3. Cook on low pressure for about 10 hours.
4. Serve and enjoy!!!

Chili with Corn, Black Beans and Ground Turkey

Preparation Time: 10 minutes

Cook Time: 3 hours

Total Time: 3 hours 10 minutes

Serves: 8

Ingredients:

- 1 Lb. ground turkey

- 1 15 Oz. can whole kernel corn

- 1 5 ½ Oz. can tomato juice

- 1 ½ Oz. package taco seasoning mix

- 1 15 Oz. can Mexican style Stewed Tomatoes

- 1 15 Oz. can black beans

Cooking Instructions:

1. In a large skillet heat the turkey to become brown and drain out extra fat.
2. Put the turkey in your Ninja Foodi. Put all other ingredients but do not drain the beans, corn or tomatoes. Stir thoroughly.
3. Cook for 3 hours on high pressure. Top with tortilla chips, low-fat sour cream, sliced green onions.
4. Serve and enjoy!!!

Boston Baked Beans

Preparation Time: 5 minutes

Cook Time: 6 hours

Total Time: 6 hours 5 minutes

Serves: 8

Ingredients:

- 1 Lb. dry white Northern beans

- ½ Tsp. black pepper

- 3 Cup of water

- 1 Cup of onion, diced fine

- 2 Slices bacon cut into small pieces

- 1 Tbsp. brown mustard

- 2 Tbsp. ketchup

- ¼ Cup of brown sugar

- ¼ Cup of dark molasses

- ½ Tsp. salt

Cooking Instructions:

1. In a large container, soak beans in water overnight. Drain and rinse.
2. Put all ingredients into Ninja Foodi.
3. Cook on low Pressure for about 6 hours.
4. Serve and enjoy!!!

VEGETARIAN RECIPES

Saffron, Courgette and Herb Couscous

Preparation Time: 10 minutes

Cook Time: 20 minutes

Total Time: 30 minutes

Serves: 8

Ingredients:

- ½ Tsp. freshly ground black pepper

- ¼ Tsp. ground cumin

- 285g Couscous

- 20g Basil leaves, chopped

- ½ Tsp. saffron threads

- 2 Tbsp. olive oil

- 30g Unsalted butter

- 2 Courgettes, large dice

- 20g Parsley leaves, chopped

- 350ml Homemade chicken stock

- 1 Tsp. salt

Cooking Instructions:

1. In a small saucepan, boil the chicken stock. Off the heat put pepper, cumin, salt, and saffron threads. Keep it steep for about 15 minutes.
2. In a sauce pan, heat the olive oil and melt the butter. Put the courgette and cook for 5 minutes. Boil the chicken stock again.
3. In a large bowl, put the couscous and the cooked courgette. Pour the hot chicken stock on top of the couscous mixture.

4. Close the bowl firmly with plastic wrap and keep it for about 15 minutes. Put the basil and parsley. Stir with fork.
5. Serve and enjoy!!!

Potato Soup

Preparation Time: 10 minutes

Cook Time: 20 minutes

Total Time: 30 minutes

Serves: 6

Calories: 350 Kcal.

Ingredients:

- Pepper

- Shredded cheddar cheese

- 2 Stalks celery, diced

- 2 Medium carrots, diced

- 2 Cloves garlic, minced

- 1 ½ Tsp. crushed rosemary

- 2 Tbsp. unsalted butter

- ½ Large onion, diced

- 5 Cups of diced red potatoes

- ¼ Cup of flour

- 3 ½ Cups of vegetable broth

- ½ Cup heavy cream

- Salt

- Sliced green onions

Cooking Instructions:

1. Put Butter into your Ninja Foodi and Sauté. Put onions, celery, carrots, salt and pepper.
2. Cook the veggies for about 5 minutes. Stir through the cooking time. Put garlic and rosemary and cook for about 30 seconds.
3. Put potatoes, flour and mix thoroughly. Stir in broth. Close the lid and make sure the pressure release valve is set to sealing position.
4. Press Manual High Pressure and set to cook for about 9 minutes. Immediately cooking time is up, do a Quick Pressure Release.
5. With an immersion blender, puree some of the veggies and put heavy cream.
6. Top with green onions and shredded cheddar.
7. Serve and enjoy!!!

Easy Kimchi Fried Rice

Preparation Time: 10 minutes

Cook Time: 20 minutes

Total Time: 30 minutes

Serves: 4

Calories: 297 Kcal.

Ingredients:

- 4 Fried eggs
- 2 Scallions, chopped
- 1 Tbsp. cooking oil
- 1 Medium onion, diced
- 1 Medium carrot, diced
- ¼ Cup of kimchi juice
- 2 Tbsp. gochujang
- 1 Tbsp. soy sauce
- 4 Cups of cooked long-grain white rice
- 2 Tsp. sesame oil
- 2 Large garlic cloves, minced
- 1 (1-inch) Cube ginger root, minced
- 1 Cup of kimchi, chopped

Cooking Instructions:

1. In a large skillet, heat oil on a medium heat. Put onion and carrot and Sauté for about 5 minutes. Put garlic and ginger.

2. Sauté and stir continuously for about 30 seconds. Put kimchi juice, gochujang, kimchi and soy sauce into the skillet.
3. Mix thoroughly and cook for about 5 minutes Put rice to skillet and give it a proper cook. Pour in sesame oil over rice and stir properly.
4. Share onto 4 serving plates and top with fried egg and green onions.
5. Serve and enjoy!!!

Vegetarian Pulled Pork

Preparation Time: 10 minutes

Cook Time: 10 minutes

Total Time: 20 minutes

Serves: 4

Ingredients:

- 20 Oz. Young Green Jackfruit

- ½ Tsp Liquid Smoke

- 1 Tsp. Paprika

- 1 ½ Tsp. Seasoning Salt

- 1 Tsp. Garlic Powder

- ½ Tsp. Onion Powder

- Pepper

- 1 Cup of Water

- 1 Cup of BBQ sauce

Cooking Instructions:

1. Open the can and drain the young green jackfruit. Use two forks and shred the jackfruit apart to look like pulled pork.
2. Put the jackfruit into your Ninja Foodi bowl; put the seasoning salt, pepper, onion, paprika and garlic.
3. Put the 1 cup of water and BBQ sauce. Mix properly.
4. Cook on your Ninja Foodi for about 10 minutes.
5. Serve and enjoy!!!

Spicy Couscous and Vegetables

Preparation Time: 15 minutes

Cook Time: 10 minutes

Total Time: 25 minutes

Serves: 4

Ingredients:

- 1 Small courgette, halved, cut into slices

- 2 Small red peppers, diced

- 2 Tbsp. chopped coriander

- 2 Tbsp. olive oil

- ½ Lemon, grated zest and juice

- 1 Small aubergine, sliced

- Olive oil, to taste

- Salt

- ½ Tsp. sea salt

- ½ Tsp. ground roasted cumin seeds

- ½ Tsp. ground ginger

- ½ Tsp. paprika

- 60ml Orange juice

- 1 Tbsp. chopped parsley

- Freshly ground black pepper

- 1 ½ Cups of couscous

- 480ml Vegetable stock

Cooking Instructions:

1. Preheat the oven to 190° C. On a baking sheet, keep the cut vegetables, sprinkle some olive oil and salt and pepper.
2. Put into the oven and heat for about 10 minutes. Place the couscous in a bowl that is heatproof. Add all the spices and orange juice.
3. Boil the vegetable stock and pour all on top of the couscous. Cover it and keep it to marinate for about 10 minutes.
4. Put the olive oil, herbs, grated lemon zest and juice. Shred the couscous with a fork and top with the roasted vegetables.
5. Serve and enjoy!!!

Toasted Israeli Couscous with Vegetables

Preparation Time: 30 minutes

Cook Time: 30 minutes

Total Time: 1 hour

Serves: 4

Ingredients:

- 12 Spears asparagus, grilled and sliced

- 2 Large red peppers, grilled, peeled and diced

- 40g Kalamata olives, pitted and chopped

- 2 Tbsp. chopped fresh basil leaves

- Freshly ground black pepper

- 1 Courgette, halved, grilled and sliced

- 1 Yellow squash, halved, grilled and sliced

- Lemon-balsamic vinaigrette

- 225g Israeli couscous

- Salt

For the lemon-balsamic vinaigrette:

- 1 Small shallot, minced

- Freshly ground black pepper

- 190ml Extra-virgin olive oil

- 3 Tbsp. fresh lemon juice

- 1 Tsp. lemon zest

- 3 Tbsp. aged balsamic vinegar

- 1 Tbsp. red wine vinegar

- Salt

Cooking Instructions:

1. On a medium heat, heat large sauté pan on grates of the barbecue.
2. Put couscous and stir properly. Grill vegetables. On a high heat, boil ½ liters of water and put 1 Tbsp. salt.
3. Stir well and cook for sometimes. Properly drain it and put in a large bowl.
4. Put the grilled vegetables, olives, basil, vinaigrette, salt and pepper. Mix thoroughly. Keep it for about 30 minutes.
5. Serve and enjoy!!!

Charred Vegetable and Couscous Salad

Preparation Time: 5 minutes

Cook Time: 20 minutes

Total Time: 25 minutes

Serves: 6

Ingredients:

- 300g Couscous

- 1 Garlic clove

- 75ml Red wine vinegar

- A Handful of rocket leaves

- ½ Bunch fresh basil, shredded

- 6 3/4 Tbsp. extra-virgin olive oil

- Salt

- 8 Asparagus spears, peeled, cut in half

- ½ Bunch spring onions, finely chopped

- 1 Aubergine, sliced

- 1 Courgette, sliced

- 1 Red pepper, de-seeded and sliced

- A sprig of fresh thyme

- ½ Chicken stock cube

Cooking Instructions:

1. In a small mixing bowl, put the couscous. Put 300ml of water in a saucepan and put 3½ Tbsp. olive oil, thyme, garlic, half stock cube and salt.

2. When the water reaches its boiling point, pour it into the couscous. Stir thoroughly. Keep it to marinate for 10 minutes.
3. Get the bowl, remove thyme and garlic and then shred the couscous with a fork. When you see that the grains are well separated, pour it into the vegetables.
4. Put the basil and rocket.
5. Serve and enjoy!!!

APPETIZER RECIPES

Corn Casserole

Preparation Time: 10 minutes

Cook Time: 38 minutes

Total Time: 48 minutes

Serves: 3

Ingredients:

- ½ Cup of butter, melted

- 2 Eggs

- 8 ½ Oz. Jiffy cornbread mix

- 1 15 Oz. can cream-style corn

- 1 Cup of sour cream

- 1 15 Oz. can whole kernel corn, drained

Cooking Instructions:

1. Put canola spray into your Ninja Foodi.
2. Mix all the ingredients in a small mixing bowl and pour them into your Ninja Foodi.
3. Lock the lid and bake at 350°F for 38 minutes.
4. Serve and enjoy!!!

Chick-Fil-A Nuggets

Preparation Time: 10 minutes

Cook Time: 12 minutes

Total Time: 22 minutes

Serves: 3

Ingredients:

- 1 Cup of milk

- 1 Cup of dill pickle juice

- 1 Tsp. paprika

- 3 Tbsp. butter, melted

- 2 Gallon size Ziploc bags

- 1 Large egg

- 1 ½ Cups all-purpose flour

- 3 Tbsp. confectioner's sugar

- 1 Lb. of chicken breast, cut into 1-2" cubes

- 2 ½ Tsp. salt

- 1 ½ Tsp. black pepper

Cooking Instructions:

1. Put the chicken and dill pickle juice to a gallon size Ziploc bag. Close the bag and put in the refrigerator for about 8 hours.
2. In a small mixing bowl, put milk and egg. Remove the bag from the refrigerator, drain the chicken from pickle juice and dip into the milk mixture.
3. Put confectioner's sugar, salt, flour, pepper and paprika to Ziploc bag and then put the chicken to bag. Give it a good shake.
4. Bury the chicken into melted butter and place them in the Ninja Foodi. Cook for about 5 minutes. Confirm that the chicken is well cooked.
5. Serve and enjoy!!!

Pickles with Dill Dip

Preparation Time: 5 minutes

Cook Time: 7 minutes

Total Time: 12 minutes

Serves: 4

Calories: 384

Ingredients:

- 2 Large eggs

- 12 Pickle spears

- 1 Cup of coconut flour

- 2 ½ Oz. package pork rinds

Sauce:

- 2 Tsp. garlic powder

- ½ Tsp. pepper

- 16 Oz. sour cream

- 1 Tbsp. dried dill

- 2 Tsp. vinegar

- 1 Tsp. salt

Cooking Instructions:

1. Cut spears into half and use a paper towel to dry it. Beat the eggs into a small mixing bowl. Put coconut flour in another mall mixing bowl.
2. Mash the pork rind with a food processor to resemble breadcrumbs. In another separate mixing bowl, put the pork rind crumbs.
3. Dip pickles in the flour, in the egg mixture and then dip into pork rinds. Place the pickles into your Ninja Foodi and cook for 7 minutes.

4. Mix together dill, garlic powder, vinegar and sour cream to a mixing bowl. Mix properly.
5. Serve and enjoy!!!

Corned Beef & Cabbage

Preparation Time: 10 minutes

Cook Time: 1 hour 18 minutes

Total Time: 1 hour 28 minutes

Serves: 4

Ingredients:

- 3 Lbs. corned beef

- 1 Lb. carrots, chopped

- 4 Red potatoes, quartered

- Pickling seasoning packet

- 1 Tbsp. stone ground mustard

- 4 Cups cold water

- 1 Medium onion, quartered

- 4 Tsp. minced garlic

- 1 Cabbage, cut into 8 wedges

Cooking Instructions:

1. Wash and Rinse your corned beef and keep it to dry using a paper towel.
2. Put quartered onion, mince garlic, corned beef, 1 Tbsp. stone ground mustard and seasoning packet into your Ninja Foodi alongside with 4 cups of cold water.
3. Lock the lid and press Manual High Pressure to cook for about 90 minutes. When the cooking time is up, do a natural pressure release for about 10 minutes.
4. Cut the vegetable. Remove the cooked corned beef and half of the hot liquid and place it in a large serving bowl.
5. Put carrots, and cabbage and red potatoes into your Ninja Foodi. Lock the lid and select Manual High Pressure and set to cook for about 3 minutes.
6. Immediately the cooking time is up, do a quick pressure release for about 10 minutes. Place your corned beef into slices. Top with cabbage and carrot.
7. Serve and enjoy!!!

Football Deviled Eggs

Preparation Time: 10 minutes

Cook Time: 5 minutes

Total Time: 15 minutes

Serves: 1

Calories: 116 Kcal.

Ingredients:

- 2 Tbsp. sweet pickle juice

- 4 Tsp. spicy brown mustard

- Salt

- 12 Hard cooked eggs, peeled and sliced

- 4 Tbsp. mayonnaise

- Pepper

Cooking Instructions:

1. Put 1 cup of water into your Ninja Foodi. Put eggs into your Ninja Foodi and close the lid.
2. Select Manual High Pressure and set to cook for about 5 minutes. Immediately the cooking time is up, do a natural pressure release for about 5 minutes.
3. Using an ice bath and in batches, cool the eggs for about 5 minutes. Remove the shell of the eggs and slice lengthwise.
4. Mix the mayonnaise, pickle juice, egg yolks, mustard, salt and pepper in any food processor.
5. Put the yolk mixture on each of the egg white.
6. Serve and enjoy!!!

Lasagna Dip

Preparation Time: 10 minutes

Cook Time: 8 minutes

Total Time: 18 minutes

Serves: 1

Calories: 69 Kcal.

Ingredients:

- 2 Cups of ricotta cheese

- 2 Cups of mozzarella, shredded

- 1 ½ Ground beef

- 1 Jar (24 oz.) spaghetti sauce

Cooking Instructions:

1. Keep your Ninja Foodi on Sauté mode. Put ground beef and sauté for about 5 minutes.
2. Remove the grease. Put spaghetti sauce into the Ninja Foodi, give it a good stir and sauté for about 5 minutes.
3. Spread ricotta cheese to cover the beef mixture. Spray shredded mozzarella cheese on the top.
4. Lock the lid and cook for about 8 minutes.
5. Serve and enjoy!!!

Peanut Butter Cups

Preparation Time: 10 minutes

Cook Time: 6 minutes

Total Time: 16 minutes

Serves: 1

Ingredients:

- 1 Tube Crescent Rolls

- 8 Peanut Butter Cups

Cooking Instructions:

1. Use crescent rolls to wrap your peanut butter cups.
2. Trim the unwanted crescent dough that will not cover the peanut butter cups.
3. Put oil in your Ninja Foodi and cook for 6 minutes.
4. Serve and enjoy!!!

Ninja foodi Oreos

Preparation Time: 5 minutes

Cook Time: 5 minutes

Total Time: 10 minutes

Serves: 1

Ingredients:

- 1 Tube Crescent Rolls

- 8 Oreos

Cooking Instructions:

1. Use crescent rolls to wrap your Oreos.
2. Trim the unwanted crescent dough that will not cover the peanut butter cups.
3. Put oil in your Ninja Foodi and cook for 6 minutes.
4. Serve and enjoy!!!

Hot Bean Dip

Preparation Time: 10 minutes

Cook Time: 25 minutes

Total Time: 35 minutes

Serves: 1

Ingredients:

- 8 Oz. cream cheese, softened

- 1 16 Oz. can refried brand

- 2 Cups of Mexican cheese

- 1 ¼ Cup of sour cream

- 1 Packet taco seasoning

Cooking Instructions:

1. Mix together sour cream, cream cheese and refried beans in a large mixing bowl. Mix properly.
2. Pour in 1 cup of Mexican cheese, taco seasoning and 1 cup of salsa.
3. Flip onto an oven-safe bowl. Put 1 cup of cheese on top and cook for 25 minutes.
4. Serve and enjoy!!!

Peppermint-Vanilla Latte

Preparation Time: 10 minutes

Cook Time: 5 minutes

Total Time: 15 minutes

Serves: 7

Ingredients:

- 1 Tsp. of vanilla

- ¼ Cup of sugar

- 4 Cups of milk

- 2 Cups of coffee

- 3 Drops of peppermint extract

Cooking Instructions:

1. Put all the ingredients into Ninja Foodi and cook on high pressure for about 5 minutes.
2. Immediately the cooking time is up, do a natural pressure release for about 10 minutes.
3. Serve and enjoy!!!

DESSERT RECIPES

Christmas tree Brownies

Preparation Time: 5 minutes

Total Time: 5 minutes

Serves: 2

Ingredients:

- Brownies baked in a square pan

- Christmas light sprinkles

- Star sprinkles

- Green food coloring

- Piping bag or zip top storage bag

- Green decorating sugar

- Premade vanilla icing

Cooking Instructions:

1. Cut the brownies on a cutting board into half and then cut triangles out of each side.
2. Do not bother about the 4 edge pieces. Mix the green food coloring into the premade vanilla icing.
3. Mix it according to your desired color. Put icing in a zip-lock bag and put the icing on each brownie.
4. Top with green decorating sugar and Christmas light sprinkles. Top each tree with a star sprinkle.
5. Serve and enjoy!!!

Baked Drunken Apples

Preparation Time: 10 minutes

Cook Time: 5 hours 30 minutes

Total Time: 5 hours 40 minutes

Serves: 4

Ingredients:

- 7 medium sized apples

- 1 cup ginger ale soda

- 1/3 cup walnuts, chopped

- ½ cup whiskey

- Cinnamon

- 1 cup brown sugar

- 1/3 cup raisins

Cooking Instructions:

1. Make a core on your apples, halfway and poach the apples in your Ninja Foodi. Combine together raisins, brown sugar and walnuts and pour them into the apples.
2. Pour in whiskey and ginger ale into walnut mixture and mix thoroughly. Pour the mixture on the apples.
3. Sprinkle the apples with cinnamon. Put them into your Ninja Foodi and cook on low heat for about 5 hours 30 minutes.
4. Serve and enjoy!!!

Pumpkin Cake

Preparation Time: 10 minutes

Cook Time: 50 minutes

Total Time: 1 hour

Serves: 2

Ingredients:

- 1 Yellow cake mix
- 1 Tbsp. pumpkin pie spice
- ½ Bag dark chocolate chips
- 1 Can pumpkin
- 1 Cup of dried cranberries

Cooking Instructions:

1. Combine together all the ingredients.
2. Put the batter to your Ninja Foodi pan. Keep it on the rack.
3. Set your Ninja Foodi oven to 350°F.
4. Bake for about 50 minutes. Do not put water.
5. Serve and enjoy!!!

Apple Cobbler

Preparation Time: 10 minutes

Cook Time: 25 minutes

Total Time: 35 minutes

Serves: 2

Ingredients:

- 2 Cups of flour

- Cinnamon

- 2 Tbsp. of butter, melted

- 2 Cups of apples, diced

- 2 Cups of milk

- 2 Cups of sugar

- Vanilla

Cooking Instructions:

1. Except the apples, combine all the ingredients together.
2. Put into your Ninja Foodi pan.
3. Put apples into the mixture.
4. Set your Ninja Foodi oven to 350°F and cook for about 25 minutes.
5. Serve and enjoy!!!

Banana Cupcakes

Preparation Time: 10 minutes

Cook Time: 20 minutes

Total Time: 30 minutes

Serves: 1

Ingredients:

- 3 Large bananas

- 1 Box of cake mixture

Cooking Instructions:

1. Preheat your Ninja Foodi at 350°F.
2. Mash the bananas and put the cake mixture.
3. Give it a good stir. Pour into cupcake pan.
4. Keep the pan on rack. Close the lid.
5. Bake 20 minutes.
6. Serve and enjoy!!!

Black Bean Brownies

Preparation Time: 10 minutes

Cook Time: 20 minutes

Total Time: 30 minutes

Serves: 1

Ingredients:

- 15 Oz can undrained black beans

- 1 Box brownie mixture

Cooking Instructions:

1. Mix the ingredients together.
2. Put them into your Ninja Foodi pan.
3. Bake for about 20 minutes.
4. Serve and enjoy!!!

Blueberry Lemon Thyme Crisp

Preparation Time: 10 minutes

Cook Time: 40 minutes

Total Time: 50 minutes

Serves: 1

Ingredients:

- Corn starch

- Pre-packaged Blueberry granola

- 1 Cup of fresh blueberries

- 5 Tsp. Sugar

- 1 Lemon

- 5 Tsp. Thyme

Cooking Instructions:

1. In a small saucepan, mix together sugar, blueberries and thyme. Cook until they are well mixed.
2. Put corn starch to thicken. Put Pam in your baking pan and pour in the ingredients.
3. Put granola into a bowl alongside with 5 pieces of butter. Mix properly.
4. Pour the mixture on the blueberries.
5. Put them in the Ninja Foodi and cook for 40 minutes.
6. Serve and enjoy!!!

Cherry Dump Cake

Preparation Time: 10 minutes

Cook Time: 2 hours

Total Time: 2 hours 10 minutes

Serves: 1

Ingredients:

- 1 Box yellow cake mixture

- 1 Stick melted butter

- 21 Oz. cans cherry pie filling

Cooking Instructions:

1. Turn the cans of cherries into your Ninja Foodi.
2. Mix together the cake mixture and melted butter in a small mixing bowl.
3. Pour batter on top of cherries.
4. Select the Slow Cook High setting on your Ninja Foodi and cook for 2 hours. Top with ice cream.
5. Serve and enjoy!!!

Chocolate Cobbler

Preparation Time: 10 minutes

Cook Time: 4 hours

Total Time: 4 hours 10 minutes

Serves: 7

Ingredients:

- ¾ Cup of butter, melted

- 2 Tsp. vanilla extract

- 2½ Cups of boiling water

- ½ Cup of milk

- 3 Cups of sugar, divided

- 1 ½ Cups of self-rising flour

- ½ Cup of plus tablespoon baking cocoa, divided

Cooking Instructions:

1. Combine together flour, milk, 1½ cups of the sugar, 2 Tsp. of the cocoa and vanilla in a large mixing bowl. Pour them on the butter.
2. In another small mixing bowl, combine together the remaining sugar and cocoa. Sprinkle on top of the batter. Pour boiled water and do not stir.
3. Close the lid on the Ninja and press Slow Cook Low. Cook for 4 hours.
4. Serve and enjoy!!!

Chocolate Lava Cake

Preparation Time: 10 minutes

Cook Time: 3 hours

Total Time: 3 hours 10 minutes

Serves: 7

Ingredients:

Cake:

- 3 Eggs

- 1 Box Betty Crocker

- 1¼ Cups milk

- ½ Cup vegetable oil

Topping:

- 1 box instant chocolate pudding and pie filling mix

- 2 cups of milk

- 1 (12 oz.) bag of milk chocolate chips

Cooking Instructions:

1. Spray your cooking spray on the Ninja Foodi. Using a large mixing bowl, beat cake ingredients with any food processor and pour into your Ninja Foodi.
2. Using another medium bowl, beat pudding mixture, 2 cups of milk and mix properly.
3. Pour into your Ninja Foodi on top of the cake batter. Do not stir. Spread chocolate chips on top.
4. Close the lid and press Slow Cook Low and cook for 3 hours.
5. Serve and enjoy!!!

Lightning Source UK Ltd.
Milton Keynes UK
UKHW051046051220
374629UK00011B/753